JOHN BUCHAN

John Buchan, first Baron Tweedsmuir of Elsfield, was born in Perth, Scotland in 1875. In his youth, his father immersed him in the history, legends and myths of Scotland, and he was an avid reader, stating some years later that John Bunyan's *The Pilgrim's Progress* was a "constant companion" to him. Buchan's education was uneven, but at the age of seventeen he obtained a scholarship to study classics at Glasgow University, where he began to write poetry. His first work, *The Essays and Apothegms of Francis Lord Bacon*, was published in 1894, and a year later he enrolled at Oxford University to study law.

In 1900, Buchan moved to London, and two years later accepted a civil service post in South Africa. In the years leading up to World War I, he worked at a publishers, and also wrote *Prester John* (1910) – which later became a school reader, translated into many languages – as well as a number of biographies.

In 1915, Buchan become a war correspondent for *The Times*, and published his most well-known book, the thriller *The Thirty-Nine Steps*. After the war he became a director of the news agency Reuters.

Over the course of his life, Buchan would eventually publish some one hundred books, forty or so of which were novels, mostly wartime thrillers. In the latter part of his life he worked in politics, serving as Conservative MP for the Scottish universities and Lord High Commissioner of the Church of Scotland (1933-34). In 1935, Buchan moved to Canada, where he became the thirty-fifth Governor General of Canada. He died in 1940, aged 64.

THE LAST SECRETS

The Final Mysteries of Exploration

By JOHN BUCHAN

TO THE MEMORY OF

Brig.-Gen. CECIL RAWLING, C.M.G., C.I.E.

WHO FELL AT THE THIRD BATTLE OF YPRES

AN INTREPID EXPLORER

A GALLANT SOLDIER

AND THE BEST OF FRIENDS

PREFACE

THE first two decades of the twentieth century will rank as a most distinguished era in the history of exploration, for during them many of the great geographical riddles of the world have been solved. This book contains a record of some of the main achievements. What Nansen said of Polar exploration is true of all exploration ; its story is a " mighty manifestation of the power of the Unknown over the mind of man." The Unknown, happily, will be always with us, for there are infinite secrets in a blade of grass, and an eddy of wind, and a grain of dust, and human knowledge will never attain that finality when the sense of wonder shall cease. But to the ordinary man there is an appeal in large, bold, and obvious conundrums, which is lacking in the *minutiæ* of research. Thousands of square miles of the globe still await surveying and mapping, but most of the exploration of the future will be the elucidation of details. The main lines of the earth's architecture have been determined, and the task is now one of amplifying our knowledge of the groyning and buttresses and stone-work. There are no more unvisited forbidden cities, or unapproached high mountains, or unrecorded great rivers.

"The world is disenchanted; oversoon
Must Europe send her spies through all the land."

It is in a high degree improbable that many geographical problems remain, the solving of which will come upon the mind with the overwhelming romance of the unveilings we have been privileged to witness. The explorer's will still be a noble trade, but it will be a filling up of gaps in a framework of knowledge which we already possess. The morning freshness has gone out of the business, and we are left with the plodding duties of the afternoon.

Some of the undertakings described in these pages have not been completed. The foot of man has not yet stood on the last snows of Everest, or on the summit of Carstensz. One notable discovery I have not dealt with—the great Turfan Depression in the heart of Central Asia, far below the sea level, the existence of which was first established by the Russian, Roborowski, before the close of last century, and the details of which have been described by Sir Aurel Stein in his *Ruins of Desert Cathay* and *Serindia*. But Sir Aurel's interest was chiefly in the antiquities of the place, and the more strictly geographical results have not yet been given to the world. To-day, if we survey the continents, we find nothing of which the main features have not been already expounded. The Amazon basin might be regarded

as an exception, and only a little while ago men
dreamed of discovering among the wilds of the Bo-
livian frontier the remains, perhaps even the survival,
of an ancient civilization. It would appear that these
dreams are baseless. The late President Roosevelt
did, indeed, succeed in putting upon the map a new
river, the Rio Roosevelt, 1,500 kilometres long, of
which the upper course was entirely unknown, and
the lower course explored only by a few rubber col-
lectors—a river which is the chief affluent of the
Madeira, which is itself the chief affluent of the
Amazon. But now all the tributaries have been
traced, and though there is much unexplored ground
in the Amazon valley, it consists of forest tracts lying
between the rivers, all more or less alike in their
general character, and with nothing to repay the
explorer except their flora and fauna. Africa is now
an open book, even though many parts have been
little travelled. The map of Asia alone holds one
blank patch which may well be the last of the great
secrets—the Desert of Southern Arabia, which lies
between Yemen and Oman, 800 by 500 miles of waterless sands. Long ago there were routes athwart it,
and hidden in its recesses some great news may await
the traveller. But its crossing will be a hazardous
affair for whoever undertakes it, since he will have to
lean upon the frail reed of milk camels for food and
transport. For the rest, the problems are now of
survey and scientific enquiry rather than of exploration
in the grand manner. .

I have many acknowledgments to make. My thanks are due in the first place to Mr. Charles Turley Smith, who has contributed the chapters on Arctic and Antarctic Exploration, subjects on which he is specially equipped to write; and, in order to put the conquest of the two Poles in its proper light, has supplied a sketch of the long story of Polar exploration. I am deeply indebted to Mr. Arthur R. Hinks, the Secretary, and to Mr. Edward Heawood, the Librarian, of the Royal Geographical Society for their help and advice. I have also to express my thanks to Messrs. Constable and Company for permission to reproduce illustrations and to quote from works published by them; to Major G. H. Putnam and Messrs. Seeley, Service, and Company for the same kindness; to Major F. M. Bailey, C.I.E., the British Political Officer in Sikkim, for the story of the Brahmaputra Gorges; and to my friends of the Mount Everest Committee for their assent to my use of their beautiful photographs of that mountain.

J. B.

CONTENTS

LIST OF PLATES

LIST OF MAPS

I
LHASA

LHASA

(*Map*, p. 24.)

TILL the summer of 1904 if one had been asked what was the most mysterious spot on the earth's surface the reply would have been Lhasa. It was a place on which no Englishman had cast an eye for a hundred years and no white man for more than half a century. In our prosaic modern world there remained one city among the clouds about which no tale was too strange for belief. The greatest of mountain barriers shut it off from the south, and on the north it was guarded by leagues of waterless desert. Explorer after explorer had set out on the quest, but all had stopped short before the golden roofs of the sacred city could be seen from any hill-top. Even in early days the place had never been explored, for the visitors had been jealously watched and hurried quickly away. In the Potala might be treasures of a culture long hidden to the world, lost treatises of Aristotle, unknown Greek poems, relics, perhaps, of the mystic kingdom of

Kubla Khan, riches of gold and jewels drawn from the four corners of Asia. . . . .

And then suddenly in 1904 we went there, not as apologetic travellers taken by side paths, but as an armed force marching along the highway to the very heart of the mystery, and letting loose at once upon the world a flood of accurate knowledge. For a moment we were carried centuries away from high politics and every modern invention, and were back in the great ages of discovery : with the Portuguese in their quest for Ophir or Prester John, or with Raleigh looking for Manoa the Golden. It was impossible for the least sentimental to avoid a certain regret for the drawing back of that curtain which had meant so much to the imagination of mankind. The shrinkage of the world goes on so fast, our horizon grows so painfully clear, that the old untiring wonder which cast its glamour over the ways of our predecessors is vanishing from the lives of their descendants. With the unveiling of Lhasa fell the last stronghold of the older romance.

I

Tibet had always been a forbidden land, and, as a rule, adventurers only penetrated its fringes. Some-

where about the year 1328 a certain Friar Odoric of
Pordenone, travelling from Cathay, is said to have
entered Lhasa; and in the middle of the sixteenth
century, Fernão Mendes Pinto may have reached it.
In 1661 the Jesuits, Grueber and D'Orville, made a
journey from Peking to Lhasa, and thence by way of
Nepal into India. In the early part of the eighteenth
century there was a temporary unveiling, and a Capuchin Mission was established in the Holy City. Various Jesuits also reached the place, notably one Desideri;
and in 1730 came Samuel Van der Putte, a Doctor of
Laws of Leiden, who stayed long enough to learn the
language. In 1745 the Capuchin Mission came to an
end, and the curtain descended. In 1774 George
Bogle of the East India Company was in Tibet on a
mission from Warren Hastings, but the first Englishman did not reach Lhasa till 1811, when Thomas
Manning, of Caius College, Cambridge, a friend of
Charles Lamb, arrived and stayed for five months
on his unsuccessful journey from Calcutta to Peking.
Till 1904 Manning was the solitary Englishman who
was known for certain to have entered the sacred city,
though there was a tale of one William Moorcroft reaching the place in 1826, and living there for twelve years
in disguise. In 1844 the French missionaries, Huc

and Gabet, reached Lhasa from China, and recorded their experiences in one of the most delightful of all books of travel. They were the last Europeans to have the privilege up to the entry of the British army. But throughout the last half of the nineteenth century Indian natives in the Government service were employed in the survey of Tibet, men of the type of the Babu whom Mr. Kipling has described in *Kim*. The whole business was kept strictly secret. The agents were known only by the letters of the alphabet, and when they crossed the Tibetan borders they were aware that they had passed beyond the protection of the British Raj. More than one reached Lhasa by fantastic routes, with the result that the Indian Government had accurate information about the city filed in its archives, while the world at large knew the place only from the story of Huc and Gabet, and from the drawing of the Potala made by Grueber in the seventeenth century.

Of the later European travellers none reached the capital. Mr. Littledale in 1895 was not stopped by the Tibetan authorities till he was within fifty miles of the city, and Sven Hedin in 1901 got within fourteen days of Lhasa from the north. But meantime events were happening which were to impel the Government of India to interfere more actively in Tibetan policy than by merely sending native agents to collect news. The traditional policy was to preserve Tibet as a sanctuary, but a sanctuary is only a sanctuary if all the neighbours combine to hold it inviolate.

In 1903 the position of Britain and Tibet was like that of a big boy at school who is tormented by an impertinent youngster. He bears it for some time, but at last is compelled to administer chastisement. The Convention of 1890 and the Trade Regulations of 1893 were outraged by the Tibetans in many of their provisions ; our letters of protest were returned unopened ; and, since news travels fast upon the frontier, our protected peoples began to wonder what made the British Raj so tolerant of ill-treatment. This was bad enough for our prestige in the East, but the danger became acute when we discovered that the Dalai Lama was in treaty with Russia, and that an avowed Russian agent, one Dorjieff, was in residence at his court. The two powers in Lhasa were the Dalai Lama, who speedily fell under Russian influence, and the Tsong-du, or Council, composed of representatives of the great priestly caste, who suspected all innovations, and were in favour of maintaining the traditional policy of exclusion against Russia and Britain alike. China, though the nominal suzerain, was impotent, her Viceroy, the Amban, being partially insulted by both parties.

In these circumstances Britain could only make her arrangements by going direct to headquarters. Dorjieff had played his cards with great skill, and seemed to be winning everywhere. The Dalai Lama was wholly with him, and had received from the Tsar a complete set of vestments of a Bishop of the Greek Church. The Russian monarch was recognized as a Bodisat incarnation, representing no less a person than Tsong-kapa, the Luther of Lamaism ; and Russia was popularly believed to be a Buddhist Power, or, at any rate, the sworn protector of the Buddhist faith. It is difficult to overestimate the significance of these doings ; but at the same time Russian influence was rather potential than actual. The Cossacks who accompanied Sven Hedin were headed off from the Holy City as vigorously as any English explorer, and the tales of arming with Russian rifles which filtered through to India were rather intelligent anticipations than records of facts.

There were thus two parties in Tibet pulling against each other, but both in different ways hostile to our interests. The Dalai Lama and Dorjieff favoured a departure from the traditional Tibetan policy in favour of Russia. The Tsong-du and the Lamaist hierarchy in general were all for exclusion, but in their wilfulness declined to observe treaties or behave with neighbourly honesty. This internal strife, which alone made possible the success of our expedition, also made its dispatch inevitable, for neither party was prepared to listen to any argument but force. Few enterprises have ever been undertaken by Britain more unwillingly, and her decision was only arrived at under the compulsion of stark necessity. There were many who reprobated what they assumed to be a violation of the sacred places of an ancient, pure, and pacific religion. But there was no need for compunction on that score, since Lamaism was the grossest perversion of Buddhism in all Asia. Spiritually it had more kinship with the aboriginal devil-worship of Tibet than the gentle creed of Gautama. Practically it was a political tyranny of monks, who battened upon a mild and industrious population and ruled them with coarse theological terrors. Our reception by the monasteries was sufficiently gruff; but to the common people we came rather in the guise of friends.

In July, 1903, Colonel Younghusband, as he then was, Mr. White, and Captain O'Connor went to Khamba

Jong, a place in Southern Tibet, just north of Sikkim. There they met the Abbot of Tashilhunpo and certain emissaries from Lhasa, but nothing could be done ; and, with the concurrence of the Indian Office, it was arranged that a Mission should go to Gyangtse, the chief town of Southern Tibet, accompanied by a small escorting force. While troops were being collected, the Commissioner, Colonel Younghusband, went to Tuna, on the bleak plain above the Tang La, where he waited through three weary winter months. Meanwhile General Macdonald, a soldier who had had a distinguished record in Central Africa, took up his quarters at Chumbi, while Major Bretherton, the chief transport and supply officer, accumulated stores in that valley and prepared the line of communications. Those were anxious months of waiting for the Mission, for the Tibetans were in force in the neighbourhood, and daily threatened to attack the small post ; but nothing happened till the escort joined them in the end of March, 1904, and all things were ready for the advance.

It is worth while looking back upon the road to Tuna from the plains of Bengal, surely one of the most wonderful of the Great North Roads of the world. At Siliguri the little toy railway to Darjeeling runs up the hill-side ; but the path for the troops lay along the gorge of the Teesta River, through forests of sal and gurjun, which give place in turn to teak and bamboo, till the altitude increases and the tree-fern and rhododendron take their places, and at last the pines are reached and the fringe of the snows is near. From the glorious sub-tropical vegetation of Gangtok, the capital of Sikkim, the road runs through difficult ravines till it passes the tree-line at Lagyap and climbs over the frozen summit of the Natu La. From this point Tibet is visible, with the majestic snows of Chumulhari hanging like a cloud in the north. Then you descend to the Chumbi valley, the Debatable Land of Tibet, where stands Ta-Karpo, the great White Rock which recalls a famous passage in the *Odyssey*. Right under Chumulhari and just south of the Tang La, lies Phari Jong, the first of the minor Tibetan fortalices, which looks as if it were a bad copy of some European model. A little farther and you are over the pass and on the great plateau of Tuna, where icy winds blow from the hills and drive the gritty soil in blizzards about the traveller. There are few places in the world where in so short a time so complete a climatic and scenic change can be experienced.

II

On the 31st March the expedition left Tuna ; and after an unfortunate encounter with the Tibetans, which cost the latter many lives, and in which Mr. Edmund Candler, the distinguished war correspondent, was wounded, the enemy made a further stand at Red Idol Gorge. Nothing of importance, however, occurred till the town of Gyangtse was reached and occupied without a shot. Very soon it became apparent that no more could be done here than at Khamba Jong, and the Government of India were obliged to sanction a farther advance to Lhasa. For this preparations must be made ; so the Commissioner, with a small escort, took up his quarters at Gyangtse, while General Macdonald returned to Chumbi for reinforcements. The jong was found to be deserted, but, unfortunately, was neither held nor destroyed, the Mission residing in the plain below.

At first the waiting among those iris-clad meadows was pleasant and idyllic enough ; the country people brought abundant supplies, and members of the staff rode through the neighbourhood and had tea with various dignitaries of the Church ; but early in May things took a turn for the worse. It was reported that the Tibetans were fortifying the Karo La, the next pass on the Lhasa road ; and, since it is the first principle of frontier warfare to strike quickly, Colonel Brander was dispatched with the larger part of the garrison to disperse them. He performed the task with conspicuous success, and the incident is remarkable for one of the strangest pieces of fighting in our military history. It was necessary to enfilade a sangar in which the enemy was ensconced, and a native officer, Wassawa Singh, with twelve Gurkhas, was detached for the work. They climbed by means of cracks and chimneys up a 1,500 feet cliff—an exploit which would have done credit to any Alpine club, even if the climbers had not been cumbered with weapons, exposed to fire, and labouring at a height of nearly 19,000 feet.

During the engagement disquieting news arrived from Gyangtse that the jong had been reoccupied by the enemy and that the Mission was undergoing a continuous bombardment. Colonel Brander hurried back, to find that the world had moved fast in his absence, and that there was a new type of Tibetan army to be faced—a type possessed of both dash and persistence, with some notion of strategy, and with guns which, at short range, could do real execution.

So began the blockade of the Mission house; an imperfect blockade, for the telegraph wires remained intact, the mail was delivered with fair regularity, and the besieged endured no special privations. "The honours," says Mr. Perceval Landon,* "were pretty evenly divided. Neither the Tibetans nor we were able to storm the other's defences; a mutual fusillade compelled each side to protect its occupants by an elaborate system of traverses; and straying beyond the narrow tracts of the fortifications was, on either side, severely discouraged by the other."

An attempt to cut our communications failed, and by the capture of Pala the garrison greatly strengthened its position. Our troops had an experience of the type of fighting which has scarcely been known since the great sackings of the Thirty Years' War. In an upland country we expect attacks on fortified hilltops, and long-range encounters, such as we saw in South Africa. But in an episode like the capture of Naini, it was mediæval street fighting that we had to face. The Castle of Otranto provided no more endless labyrinths than those Tibetan monasteries. "Bands of desperate swordsmen were found in knots under trap-doors and behind sharp turnings. They

* _Lhasa_, by Perceval Landon.

would not surrender, and had to be killed by rifle shots
fired at a distance of a few feet."

On the 26th June General Macdonald arrived with
a relieving force, and soon after came the Tongsa Pen-
lop, the temporal ruler of Bhutan, a genial potentate
in rich vari-coloured robes and a Homburg hat. The
Tibetan offensive had weakened, but the jong had to
be taken before the Mission could advance. Down the
middle of the precipitous south-eastern face of the
great rock ran a deep fissure, across which walls had
been built. It was decided to breach these walls by our
gun fire and then to attack by way of the cleft. The
actual assault was a brilliant and intrepid exploit, for
which Lieutenant Grant of the 8th Gurkhas most
deservedly received the Victoria Cross. With our guns
battering the walls above, he and his men scrambled
up the ravine, while masses of rubble poured down on
them, and every now and then carried off a man.
Then the Gurkhas' bugles warned the guns to cease,
and the last climb began up a face so steep that there
was no possible shelter from the enemy's fire. By
such desperate mountaineering the invaders at last
reached the wreckage of the Tibetan wall. Grant
and one of the Gurkhas were the first two men over,
and to the observers below their death seemed a

certainty. They were two against the whole enemy force in the jong, and had the Tibetans reserved their fire and waited at the bastions, they could have picked off every man of the assault as his head appeared above the breach. But the bold course proved the wise one, and presently the garrison surrendered. Rarely has the Victoria Cross been better earned, and it is satisfactory to know that Lieutenant Grant reaped the reward of perfect fearlessness and received only a slight wound.

III

On the 14th July the expedition moved out from Gyangtse along the road to Lhasa. Grass and a glory of flowers covered the glens which led up to the Karo La. The serious fighting was over, and the second crossing of that pass was remarkable only for the fact that some rock platforms and caves had to be cleared by our panting troops at an altitude of over 19,000 feet. In the rest of the story the soldier finds little place, and the interest attaches itself to the durbars of the Commissioner and the treasure-house of natural and artistic wonders which the Mission was approaching. For after Gyangtse the resistance of the Tibetans was

at an end. Half-sullenly and half-curiously they permitted our advance, delaying us a little with fruitless
negotiations, while in Lhasa the game of high politics
which the Dalai Lama had played was turning against
him, and, like another deity, he was meditating a
pilgrimage.

After the Karo La came the Yam-dok—or, as some
call it, the Yu-tso or Turquoise Lake—the most wonderful natural feature of the plateau. Its curious shape, its
pale blue waters, its shores of white sand fringed with
dog-roses and forget-me-nots, the cloud of fable which
has always brooded over it, and its august environment, make it unique among the lakes of the world.
I quote a fragment of Mr. Landon's description :—

" Below lie both the outer and the inner lakes, this following with counter-indentations the in-and-out windings of the
other's shore-line. The mass and colour of the purple distance is Scotland at her best—Scotland, too, in the slow drift
of a slant-roofed raincloud in among the hills. At one's feet
the water is like that of the Lake of Geneva. But the tattered
outline of the beach, with its projecting lines of needle-rocks,
its wide, white curving sandspits, its jagged islets, its precipitous spurs, and, above all, the mysterious tarns strung one
beyond another into the heart of the hills, all these are the
Yam-dok's own, and not another's. If you are lucky, you
may see the snowy slopes of To-nang gartered by the waters,
and always on the horizon are the everlasting ice-fields of the
Himalayas, bitterly ringing with argent the sun and colour

of the still blue lake. You will not ask for the added glories
of a Tibetan sunset; the grey spin and scatter of a rain-threaded
afterglow, or the tangled sweep of a thundercloud's edge
against the blue, will give you all you wish, and you will have
seen the finest view in all this strange land."

On the shore lies the convent of Samding, the home
of the Dorje Phagmo, or pig goddess, which was jealously respected by the troops, since its abbess had
nursed Chundra Dass, one of the adventurous agents
of the Indian Government, when he fell sick during
his travels. The present incarnation, a little girl of
six, declined to reveal herself. Nothing was more
satisfactory in the whole tale of the expedition than
the way in which any service done at any time to a
British subject, white or black, met with full recog-
nition. Such conduct cannot have failed to have
raised the prestige of the Power which showed itself
so mindful of its servants. Prestige and reputation
of a kind, indeed, we already possessed. Tibetan
monasteries had a trick of sending their most valuable
belongings to the nearest convent, for, they argued,
the English do not enter nunneries or war with women.

On July 24th the expedition crossed the Khamba La
and descended to the broad green valley of the Tsangpo. The crossing of that river, a work of real difficulty,

View of the Potala Monastery at Lhasa

was made tragic by the death of Major Bretherton, the brilliant transport officer, to whom, perhaps, more than to any other soldier, the military success in the enterprise was due. Not the least of the mysteries of Tibet was this secret stream, which the traveller, after miles of bleak upland, finds flowing among English woods and meadows. In Assam and Bengal it was the Brahmaputra ; but when it entered the hills it was as unknown to civilized man as Alph or the Four Rivers of Eden. What its middle course was like and how it broke through the mountain barrier were questions which no one had answered,* nor at the time was there any accurate knowledge of its upper valleys.

Once on the north bank Lhasa was but a short way off, and in growing excitement the expedition covered the last stages. It was one of the great moments of life, and we can all understand and envy the final hurried miles, till through the haze the eye caught the gleam of golden roofs and white terraces. The first prospect brought no disappointment. If the streets were squalid, they were set in a green plain seamed with waters ; trees and gardens were everywhere ; while, above, the huge Assisi-like citadel of the Potala

* See Chapter II.

typified the massive secrecy of generations, and the
ring of dark hills reminded the onlooker that this
garden ground was planted on the roof of the world.

Meanwhile the expedition set itself down outside
the gates to abide the pleasure of the sullen and per-
turbed masters. The deity of the place had gone on
a journey, no one quite knew whither. He had kept
his moonlight flitting a secret, and had gone off on
the northern road with Dorjieff and a small escort
to claim the hospitality of his spiritual brother of
Urga. He had played his impossible game with spirit
and subtlety, and he had a pretty taste for romance
in its ending. "When one looks for mystery in Lhasa,"
wrote Mr. Candler, "one's thoughts dwell solely on
the Dalai Lama and the Potala. I cannot help dwell-
ing on the flight of the thirteenth incarnation. It
plunges us into mediævalism. To my mind there is
no picture so engrossing in modern history as that
exodus when the spiritual head of the Buddhist Church,
the temporal ruler of six millions, stole out of his
palace by night, and was borne away in his palanquin."

The romance which Mr. Candler saw in the Potala,
Mr. Landon found most conspicuously in the church
of the Jo-kang. The palace was magnificent from
the outside, but within it was only a warren of small

rooms and broken stairways. The great cathedral, on the other hand, was hidden away among trees and streets, so that its golden roof could only be seen from a distance, but inside it was a shrine of all that was mysterious and splendid. The contrast was allegorical of the difference between the temporal ruler of Lamaism—gaudy, tyrannical, and hollow—and the sway of the Buddhist Church, which by hidden ways and unseen agencies dominated the imagination of Asia. The Chinese Amban, having a natural desire to pay back the people who had so grossly neglected him, invited certain members of the Mission to enter this Holy of Holies. The visitors were the first white men to approach the inner sanctuary of the Buddhist faith. They were stoned on leaving the building, but the sight was one worth risking much to see. In the central shrine sat the great golden Buddha, roped with jewels, crowned with turquoise and pearl, surrounded by dim rough-hewn shapes which loomed out fitfully in the glare of the butter-lamps, while the maroon-clad monks droned their eternal chant before the silver altar. And the statue was as strange as its environment.

" For this is no ordinary presentation of the Master. The features are smooth and almost childish ; beautiful they are not, but there is no need of beauty here. There is no trace of that inscrutable smile which, from Mukden to Ceylon, is inseparable from our conception of the features of the Great Teacher. Here there is nothing of the saddened smile of the Melancholia, who has known too much and has renounced it all as vanity. Here, instead, is the quiet happiness and the quick capacity for pleasure of the boy who had never yet known either pain, or disease, or death. It is Gautama as a pure and eager prince, without any thought for the morrow or care for to-day."

Mr. Landon has other pictures of almost equal charm. He takes us to the famous Ling-kor, the sacred road which encircled the town, worn with the feet of generations of men seeking salvation. We see the unclean abode of the Ragyabas, that strange unholy caste of beggar scavengers ; we walk in the gardens of the Lu-kang, by the willow-fringed lake and the glades of velvet turf ; and, not least, we visit the temple of the Chief Wizard, where every form of human torment is delicately portrayed in fresco and carving. But if we wish to realize the savagery at the heart of this proud theocracy, we must go with Mr. Candler to the neighbouring Depung monastery on the quest for supplies, and see the tribe of inquisitors buzzing out like angry wasps, and submitting only when the guns were trained on them. For these weeks of waiting in Lhasa were an anxious time for all concerned. Our own position was precarious in the extreme, and, had the Lhasans once realized it, impossible. Winter was approaching, the Government was urging the Mission to get its Treaty and come home, and yet day after day had to pass without result, and the Commissioner could only wait, and oppose to the obstinacy of the monks a stronger and quieter determination. Sir Francis Younghusband was indeed almost the only man in the Empire fitted for the task. "He sat through every durbar," says Mr. Candler, " a monument of patience and inflexibility, impassive as one of their own Buddhas. Priests and councillors found that appeals to his mercy were hopeless. He, too, had orders from his King to go to Lhasa; if he faltered, *his* life also was at stake ; decapitation would await *him* on his return. That was the impression he purposely gave them. It curtailed palaver. How in the name of all their Buddhas were they to stop such a man ? "

At last on 1st September, when after a month's diplomacy the Tibetans had only admitted two of our demands, the time came to deliver our ultimatum. The delegates were told that if all our terms were not accepted within a week, General Macdonald would consider the question of using stronger arguments.

Our forbearance was justified by its results, for the opposition suddenly subsided, and we gained what we asked without any coercion. It was a diplomatic triumph of a high order, obtained in the face of difficulties which seemed to put diplomacy out of the question. The final scene came on 7th September, when in the audience chamber of the Potala the Treaty was signed by the Commissioner, and by the acting Regent, who affixed the seal of the Dalai Lama, the four Shapés, a representative of the Tsong-du, and the heads of the great monasteries. Thereafter came a limelight photograph of the gathering, and with this very modern climax the great Asian mystery became a thing of the past. The Dalai Lama had already been formally deposed, his spiritual powers were transferred to our friend the Tashe Lama, and, with the Treaty in our baggage and a real prestige in our wake, we began the homeward march.

IV

What were the results of the expedition ? Geographically they appeared a little barren, for we stuck too close to the highroad to solve many of the greater mysteries. One fact of cardinal importance was established : our conception of Tibet was revolutionized, and instead of an arid plateau we learned that about one-third of it was nearly as fertile and well-watered as Kashmir. For the rest, the two most interesting expeditions were forbidden—down the Brahmaputra to Assam, and to the mountains, nine days north of Lhasa, which had formed the southern limit of Sven Hedin's exploration. One valuable expedition was, however, undertaken. Western Tibet had hitherto been the best known part of the tableland, and now our knowledge of it was linked on to the Lhasan district. On 10th October Captains Ryder, Rawling, and Wood, and Lieutenant Bailey,* with six Gurkhas, left Gyangtse, and made their way by Shigatse up the Tsangpo. They explored the river to its source, and, passing the great Manasarowar lakes, arrived at Gartok, on the Upper Indus. Thence they entered the Sutlej valley, and, crossing the Shipki Pass of over 18,000 feet, reached Simla in the first week of January 1905. Much was added also to our knowledge of the Himalaya. The fact was established that the old report of northern rivals to Everest was unfounded ; and, moreover, the highest mountain in the world was seen from the northern side, where

* See Chapter II.

the slopes are easier, and the possibility of an attempt on it occurred to various minds—a hope which seventeen years later was realized.*

On the political side the true achievement was not the formal Treaty, but the going to Lhasa. We taught the Tibetans that their mysterious capital could not be shut against our troops, and that Russian promises were less real than British performances. We showed ourselves strong, and, above all things, humane, and we earned respect, and, it would also appear, a kind of affection. When the venerable Regent solemnly blessed the Commissioner and General Macdonald for their clemency, and presented each with a golden image of Buddha—an honour rarely granted to the faithful, and never before to an unbeliever—he gave expression to the general feeling of the people.

Tibet was enveloped once more in its old seclusion —a deeper seclusion, indeed, since we guaranteed it. A final result was that we vindicated our claim to protect our subjects and those who served us. We took our Gurkhas into the forbidden land, which their native traditions had invested with a miraculous power, and showed them the truth. As for Bhutan, up to 1904 it was as obscure as Tibet and its people were strangers.

* See Chapter IX.

They were now, in the Commissioner's phrase, " our enthusiastic allies." Their ruler in his Homburg hat joined us in the march, and acted as master of ceremonies in introducing us to the Lhasa notables.

Nearly twenty years have passed, and much water has since run under the bridges. In 1906 China adhered to the Treaty, and in 1907 came the Anglo-Russian Convention which provided for the secluding of the country by both Powers, and recognized China's suzerain rights. In 1909 the Dalai Lama, who had been restored, was ejected by Chinese troops, and in 1910 he was at Darjeeling, a refugee claiming our hospitality. Once again he was reinstated, and he has ever since been a faithful ally of Britain. At the outbreak of the Great War he offered 1,000 Tibetan troops, and informed the King that lamas through the length and breadth of Tibet were praying for the success of the British arms and for the happiness of the souls of the fallen.

Since 1904 both China and Russia have crumbled into anarchy. There is no peril to India through the eastern Himalayan passes, and the strategic importance of Tibet has dwindled. It is still a forbidden country, but it is no longer a secret one. Posts run regularly to Lhasa, and a telegraph line has been laid

to that mysterious capital. But it is mysterious only
by a literary convention. The true mystery is gone ;
the secret, such as it was, has been revealed, and the
human mind can no longer play with the unknown.
Childe Roland had reached the dark tower and found
it not so marvellous after all. It is hard not to sym-
pathize with Mr. Candler's plaint : " There are no
more forbidden cities which men have not mapped
and photographed. Our children will laugh at modern
travellers' tales. They will have to turn again to
Gulliver and Haroun al Raschid. And they will soon
tire of these. For now that there are no real mysteries,
no unknown land of dreams, where there may still
be genii and mahatmas and bottle-imps, that kind
of literature will be tolerated no longer. Children
will be sceptical and matter-of-fact and disillusioned,
and there will be no sale for fairy stories any more.
But we ourselves are children. Why could we not
have left at least one city out of bounds ? "

These reflections do not detract from the romance
of the expedition itself and the privilege of the fortunate men who shared in it. For them it was
assuredly a great adventure—one which could never
be repeated. It may be summed up, as Mr. Landon
has summed it up, in certain famous lines from the

Odyssey which have not only a curious local appli-
cation, but embody the true spirit of the adventure :—

" Over the tides of Ocean on they pressed,
 On past the great White Rock beside the stream,
On, till, through God's high bastions east and west,
They reached the plains with pale-starred iris dressed,
And found at last the folk of whom men dream."

II

THE GORGES OF THE BRAHMAPUTRA

THE GORGES OF THE BRAHMAPUTRA

(*Map*, p. 48.)

FIFTY years ago one of the questions most debated among geographers was the origin of the Brahmaputra. The great river, navigable for 800 miles from its mouth, was familiar enough in its course through the plains of India ; but it flowed from the wild Abor country, and no part of the Indian borders was less known than those north-eastern foothills. Meantime in Tibet, north of the main chain of the Himalayas, there was a large river, the Tsangpo, flowing from west to east. Did the Tsangpo ultimately become the Brahmaputra, or did it flow into the Irrawadi, or even into the Yang-tse Kiang ? All three views were held, but there was no evidence to decide between them.

In 1874 a native explorer, the pundit Nain Singh, started on his famous journey from Leh to Lhasa, and was instructed, if possible, to follow the Tsangpo and see where it went. He reached Lhasa, and on his return struck the Tsangpo at Tsetang, well to the east of the point where the British expedition crossed in 1904. He followed its course for thirty miles farther down, but was prevented from continuing his journey and compelled to return by the direct route to India. In 1878 another native explorer, G.M.N., seems to have followed the Tsangpo down as far as Gyala, which is not far from the point where the river turns sharply to the south, but his reports were not considered reliable. In 1884 another native, Kinthup, succeeded in following the Tsangpo to a point called Pemako-chung. There he found an enormous gorge, and was compelled to make a detour out to the north and east, rejoining the stream where it entered the Abor country. Kinthup's report was of the highest interest. He had stood at the beginning of an apparently impassable gorge, and he reported a fall at Pemakochung of 150 feet. He was, however, quite illiterate and was only able to make his report from memory, and it presently appeared that the height might be only 50 feet, and that the higher fall was not in the main stream but in a small tributary. One fact, however, of the utmost importance had been established by his expedition. The Tsangpo was beyond reasonable doubt the Brahmaputra in its upper course.

The Lhasa expedition in 1904 would fain have traced

the river to the plains had not the Government inter-
posed a veto.   In the years that followed, the source
of the Tsangpo was discovered by Captain Rawling.
In 1911 the Abor expedition increased our knowledge
of the course of the Brahmaputra right up to the skirts
of the main range.   The problem now was not the
linking up of the Tsangpo and the Brahmaputra, but
what happened to the river in the hairpin bend between Pemakochung and its debouchment in the
Abor valleys.   The elevation of the stream at the
point where ` the main road to Lhasa crossed it
was in the neighbourhood of 12,000 feet.   From
there as far as Pemakochung we knew that there was
no very great loss in altitude, but when the Brahmaputra appeared in the Abor foothills it was only
between 1,000 and 2,000 feet above the sea.   The
stretch of unknown course was perhaps 200 miles,
and in that section the river broke through the main
range of the Himalaya.   It was possible—nay, it was
probable—that somewhere in those gorges, which
Kinthup had thought impassable, lay hidden the most
tremendous waterfall in the world.

The secret of the Brahmaputra gorges was one of
the topics that most fascinated geographers between
the years 1904 and 1913.   In that latter year the

mystery was solved, and the *ignotum* proved not to be the *magnificum*. This is the story of the solution.

The course of the Brahmaputra through Assam is roughly from north-east to south-west, but at a place called Sadiya the main stream, there known as the Dihang, turns sharply to the north. At that point, too, it receives an important tributary on its left bank called the Dibang. During the winter of 1912–13 Captain F. M. Bailey, an officer of the Indian Political Service, was employed by the Government to survey the Dibang basin, while another party had gone through the Abor country to survey the Dihang. Early in 1913 Captain Bailey and Captain Morshead of the Royal Engineers collected what stores they could and started off from the village of Mipi on the upper waters of the Dibang. Their aim was to cross into the Dihang valley, and to follow the river upstream to the Tibetan plateau. Captain Bailey had been with the Lhasa expedition, and had had a long record of exploration in different parts of Tibet, so he had all the qualifications needed by the pioneer. But his party was imperfectly equipped, since it started more or less on the spur of the moment, and had no time to obtain proper stores from India. He trusted to the prestige won by the Abor expedition, and his experience of the ways of the Tibetans, to furnish him with coolies and local supplies.

The reader's attention is now prayed for the map. The first business was to cross the high passes separating the Dibang from the Dihang. The weather proved abominable, and for part of the route only half rations could be issued. As they descended into the valley of the Dihang they found once more cultivation and villages, and they were able to supplement their stores by shooting game, especially pheasants, which teemed by the roadside. It was necessary to establish touch with the Abor Survey party lower down the river, and accordingly they had to halt for some days. At a place called Kapu they managed to take the altitude in the river bed, and found the height above sea level to be 2,610 feet—an important result, for they were able to take no other observation at water level below the main gorges.

These foothills of the Himalaya were inhabited chiefly by savage tribes akin to the Abors, who were known generically as Lopas. But as the expedition advanced up the river they came to the country of the Pobas, who were under Tibetan influence. At Lagung, which is about the centre of the hairpin bend, the course of the river turned west. It might have been possible for them to have followed it some thirty miles farther, but they were pressed by a Poba official, with whom they made friends, to go north-east into the absolutely unknown country of Po-me, which would enable them to make a circuit and reach Gyala at the head of the gorges. Captain Bailey considered that it would be easier to explore the gorges by going downstream.

On 21st June they crossed a pass of over 13,000 feet into the valley of the river known as the Po-Tsangpo, an affluent of the Brahmaputra. It was a stream 80 yards wide, and of such rapidity that its current was one whirl of foam. The natives were in great fear of the Chinese, and it was necessary to go boldly to Showa, the capital, where a letter could be received from the Abor Survey party vouching for their respectability. The Chinese had burned the place, killed the chief, and decapitated the council, and the inhabitants looked askance at the travellers because of the Chinese writing on a tablet of Indian ink which they carried. After three days, however, a letter arrived from the Abor party, which persuaded them that Captain Bailey and Captain Morshead were at any rate servants of the English King.

The explorers now moved north-eastwards down the Po-Tsangpo, finding great difficulty in crossing the tributaries, where the bridges had mostly been destroyed. It was a beautiful land, bright with primula, iris, and blue poppy, and the roads were lined with raspberries. They were now leaving the Po-me country and travelling among a more civilized type of Tibetan, who wore hats like clergymen, made out of yak's hair. After crossing a pass of over 15,000 feet they returned to the main stream of the Tsangpo. This country was under the charge of Tzongpen of Tsela, who came to meet the travellers—an urbane gentleman whose son was at Rugby and a promising cricketer.

They were now on the Tsangpo above the mysterious gorges. They had left behind them the hot valleys of the lower stream and found a dry Tibetan dale, where the chief crops were barley and buckwheat. The river was broad and slow, at one point stretching into a lake 600 yards wide, and its altitude was 9,680 feet. The problem was now to follow it down from that point to the point of their last observation, where the altitude was only 2,610 feet. Somewhere in the intervening tract of gorge it must make the enormous descent of over 7,000 feet.

The first stage was the twenty-two miles down to

Gyala, which had been visited in 1878. The stream was in flood owing to melting snows, and the water-side track was difficult. Four days' march below Gyala they reached Pemakochung, the limit of Kinthup's exploration. So far they had passed various small rapids, but nothing in the nature of a fall. A mile below Pemakochung they came on Kinthup's cascade. It proved to be only some 30 feet high and not vertical.

The road now became extraordinarily intricate. Great spurs ran down to the river and blocked the glen, and it was necessary to cut paths through dense forest and thickets of rhododendron to surmount them. There was no track of any kind, and the tributaries descending from the adjacent glaciers were often hard to cross. They ran short of food, and could get no reliable information as to the possibility of their descending the stream. Captain Morshead and the coolies accordingly returned to Gyala, and Captain Bailey, with one man and fifteen pounds of flour, attempted to descend the Tsangpo by the route which a party of Monbas was said to have recently taken. He found the Monbas, but they were wild and suspicious and far from helpful. They refused to take him to their village, and declined to show him the road round the difficult cliffs. Apparently they considered that a traveller who had only one servant, and who carried most of his baggage himself, must be a person of small importance and not worth troubling about. He managed, however, to pick up from them certain news about the lower valley.

He returned to Gyala and rejoined Captain Morshead, and they proceeded to piece their knowledge together. At Gyala a small stream drops from the cliffs, making a waterfall, in which the god Shingche Chogye is concealed. The image of the deity is carved or painted in the rock behind the fall, but it is only possible to see it in winter when there is little water. This, apparently, was Kinthup's fall of 150 feet. Now, why should so meagre a natural feature have attained such celebrity among the Tibetans, for the fame of it had spread far and wide over the country? The reason seems to be that it is unique, because there are no other high falls. Had this deduction been made from Kinthup's evidence, the mystery of the Brahmaputra gorges would have been solved long ago.

The travellers collected their observations on the altitude of the river level and the speed of the current. At Pe, where they had first struck the Tsangpo, the height was 9,680 feet; thirty-four miles below it the river level was 8,730 feet, giving a drop of 28 feet a mile. At Pemakochung the altitude was 8,380 feet, and the drop 24 feet a mile. Three miles farther down the altitude was 8,090, giving a drop of 97 feet a mile, which included the 30-feet drop of Kinthup's fall. At the lowest point Captain Bailey reached in the river bed the altitude was 7,480 feet, giving a drop of 48 feet a mile. The next point on the river which they had visited was Lagung, below the gorges, where they could not take an observation in the river bed ; but forty-five miles downstream the altitude was 2,610 feet.

There remained, therefore, some fifty miles of gorge which had not been, and could not be, explored, and the information about it was only indirect. From Lagung upstream to where the Po-Tsangpo joined the Tsangpo, lay a stretch which many natives had visited. The altitude of the junction was estimated at 5,700 feet, which would give a drop of 3,090 feet in the seventy-five miles down to their observation of 2,610 feet—a fall of some 41 feet per mile. Here there was clearly no waterfall. From the junction of the two streams to the point where Captain Bailey turned back was not more than twenty miles, and the drop 1,780 feet, giving a fall of 89 feet a mile. The Monbas whom he met told him that they had hunted on the right bank of the stream throughout this unknown stretch, and that, though there were many rapids, there were no big cascades.

We are not concerned with the rest of the journey of Captain Bailey and Captain Morshead, which took them upstream to Tsetang, where Nain Singh had gone in 1874, and back to India by the wild country of the Bhutan border. Their evidence may be considered to have finally solved the riddle of how the great river breaks through the highest range on the globe. It does it by means of a hundred miles of marvellous gorges, where the stream foams in rapids, but there is no fall more considerable than can be found in many a Scottish salmon river. I am not sure that the reality is not more impressive than the romantic expectation. The mighty current is not tossed in spray over a great cliff, but during the æons it has bitten a deep trough through that formidable rock wall. Curiously enough, the rivers which break through the Himalaya chose the highest parts of the range through which to cut. South of Pemakochung is the great peak of Namcha Barwa, 25,445 feet high ; north of it is the peak of Gyala Peri, 23,460 feet. The distance between these mountains is only some fourteen miles, and through this gap, at an altitude of just under 9,000 feet, flows the great river.

III

THE NORTH POLE

THE NORTH POLE

(*Map*, p. 80.)

I

WHEN sceptical people say that Polar exploration has been of no benefit to mankind, it is permissible to think that their judgment is as unsound as their point of view is limited. Not only have Polar explorers added enormously to the scientific knowledge of the world, but they have also materially aided commerce. But even if these voyages had been barren of scientific and commercial results, they would have been infinitely worth making.

For among Polar explorers are many men who must be universally regarded as heroes. No training was more rigorous and dangerous, no work has ever called for more endurance, resource, and courage. A nation which is without its heroes is in a sad plight; a nation which has them and ignores their example can only be looked upon with pity. The spirit of high adventure is one that no country can afford to neglect.

The history of geographical discovery is, in its initial stages, almost solely one of conquest. Men, either for their own or their country's profit—and sometimes for both—went out in search of unknown lands because they wanted to trade with them. Pytheas, who has been described as " one of the most intrepid explorers the world has ever seen," was the first man to bring news of the Arctic regions to the civilized world. He did not pretend to have visited them, but in or about 330 B.C. he set out from Marseilles and journeyed north. During this voyage, which must have lasted for several years, he visited Britain, and then, proceeding to the most northerly point of the British Isles, he heard of an Arctic land called Thule, which at one time of the year enjoyed perpetual day, and at another had to endure perpetual night.

With a leap over a few hundred years we come to Ptolemy, whose influence on geography was almost paramount from the second century to comparatively modern times. No one is more dangerous than a bad cartographer, or more valuable than a good one ; but although Ptolemy made many mistakes, he also did such splendid work that it is quite easy to forget them. To him we owe the names of latitude and longitude, and it has been well said of him that he held the extraordinary "distinction of being the greatest authority on astronomy and geography for over fifteen hundred years." Ptolemy's work may have required to be corrected and amplified, but, at least, he gave the world something which was worthy of correction.

In the eighth and ninth centuries the Norsemen became terrors in Europe. "Harold of the fair hair" reigned from 860 to 930 A.D., and these seventy years formed a period of great adventure. During Harold's reign the Norsemen colonized Iceland, and in 983 Erik the Red founded a colony in Greenland, which flourished until the Norwegians ceased to take an interest in it.

Not until the fifteenth century did English seamen begin to turn their attention to the North. They were more or less forced to do so. Portugal and Spain were all-powerful in the East and West, and so England began earnestly to think of discovering a way to Cathay and the Spice Islands by a northern route. But if we were a little slow in beginning to pay attention to the Arctic regions, we have every cause to be satisfied with our work after we had once begun it. The fifteenth century saw considerable activity as regards Scandinavia, but it was not until 1505 that a charter was granted to the Company of Merchant Adventurers, and from that year we can date our real interest in Arctic discovery.

It is well, perhaps, to bear in mind, while thinking of Polar exploration, that there is a marked difference between the two Polar regions. The Arctic is an ocean surrounded by continental lands ; the Antarctic is a continental land surrounded by oceans.

In 1553 Sir Hugh Willoughby set out to try and find a north-east passage to the Indies. On this voyage—in which Willoughby lost his life—Novaya Zemlya was discovered, and Richard Chancellor, who took part in the expedition, reached Archangel; and then, travelling overland to Moscow, was received graciously by Ivan the Terrible, the Tsar of Russia. This visit was of importance, because it helped to establish trade between England and Russia.

Competition to find a route northwards to China and the Indies had by this time become acute in Europe, and many bold navigators set out from England. Among the sailors who were maintaining her high record on the seas Sir Martin Frobisher deserves especially to be mentioned. In 1576 he set out, cheered doubtless by knowing that Queen Eliza-

beth had "good liking of their doings," to find a
north-west passage. On three occasions Frobisher
voyaged northwards, and he reached Greenland and
discovered the strait that was named after him.
"He is not worthy," Sir Humphrey Gilbert wrote in
the latter part of the sixteenth century, "to live at
all who, for fear of danger or death, shunneth his
country's service or his own honour, since death is
inevitable, and the fame of virtue immortal." Most
assuredly our Elizabethan sailors did not shun their
"country's service," and Elizabeth herself was the
first to appreciate and encourage their enterprise.

In 1585 yet another distinguished explorer, John
Davis, embarked upon his career, and during his
voyages he made discoveries that "converted the
Arctic regions from a confused myth into a defined
area." He found several passages towards the west,
and thus strengthened the hope of finding a north-
west passage; and he also reached "the farthest
north," 72° 12' N., some eleven hundred miles from
the geographical North Pole.

As yet no one had turned his thoughts to the North
Pole itself, but it may truly be said that Davis and
men of his calibre were already beginning to prepare
the way for the time when it would be reached. For

his discoveries, like those of many of the earlier explorers, were both important in themselves and also acted as a guide and incentive to those who followed. In the meantime, Davis had obtained the record for the "farthest north," a record which Great Britain, with the exception of a very few years, continued to hold until 1882.

Many English navigators did great work in maintaining this record, and among them was Henry Hudson, who set out in 1607 with the object of finding a north-west passage to the Indies. Hudson, in this voyage, reached 80° N., and did most valuable work in the Spitzbergen quadrant. It is also reported that two of his men saw a mermaid, which may at least be taken as evidence that they were more than ordinarily observant. Both geographically and commercially, Hudson's voyages were of the first importance. He not only made many discoveries, including that of the river which bears his name, but he also brought back the news that led directly to the establishment of the Spitzbergen whale fishery, an industry that was extremely lucrative to Holland.

In 1615 William Baffin discovered the land that is called after him; and then, for some time, English discovery in the Arctic regions ceased to be noteworthy. Baffin made no less than five voyages to the North, and, scientifically, his observations were permanently valuable to subsequent explorers.

Apart from geographical discovery, these Arctic voyages had so far been a great stimulant to trade. In Greenland, Davis Strait, and the Spitzbergen seas, trade had followed discovery, and what had happened in those parts of the Arctic also took place in Hudson Bay, after the Hudson's Bay Company was formed in 1668. In fact, for the time being, the desire to make geographical discoveries was almost obliterated by the desire to trade.

It is, however, pleasant to note that during the eighteenth century some of our Governments took an intelligent interest in geographical discovery. They offered a reward of £5,000 for reaching 89° N., and £20,000 was offered to any one who could find the North-West Passage. In the earlier part of the eighteenth century the part that the Russians took in Arctic discovery must not be omitted. In 1728 Peter the Great sent out an expedition under the command of Vitus Bering, a Dane, in which Bering Strait and other discoveries were made ; and although it is impossible to mention them in detail, the contributions that the Russians made in revealing the New

World to the Old were most creditable to them as a nation.

In 1773 Captain Phipps conducted an expedition, which now derives its chief interest from the fact that Horatio Nelson, then a young midshipman, took part in it. "Great," says Sir Clements Markham, " as are the commercial advantages obtained from Arctic discovery, and still greater as are its scientific results, the most important of all are its uses as a nursery for our seamen, as a school for our future Nelsons, and as affording the best opportunities for distinction to young naval officers in time of peace." And it is incontestably true that many of our finest sailors have learnt their trade in the severe school of geographical exploration.

With the advent of the nineteenth century many expeditions were sent to the Far North. The desire actually to reach the North Pole itself did not enter the thoughts of these courageous navigators, the main object of their voyages being either to find the North-West Passage round North America to the Indies, or the North-East Passage round Asia. Nevertheless, each one of these voyages added to the store of knowledge that was being accumulated, each expedition solved some of the mysteries of the North and prepared the way for the solution of what came to be considered *the* greatest mystery of all.

In 1819 Sir Edward Parry embarked upon the first of the Arctic voyages which have made his name famous in the annals of exploration. A sailor by profession, Parry was happy in possessing the qualities that fitted him to lead men. During his first expedition, the prize offered by the English Government to the first navigator who passed the 110th meridian was won. Parry and his party spent a winter in the Arctic—a winter which, thanks to their leader's careful preparations, was passed without mishap ; and then, when the winter was over, an expedition to explore the interior of Melville Island was made. Thus Arctic travelling was inaugurated by Parry.

Other successful voyages under the same leadership followed, and when, in 1827, our Admiralty began favourably to consider the idea of getting as near as possible to the Pole by way of Spitzbergen, Parry was naturally chosen to command the expedition. So, for the fourth time, Parry sailed northwards, and having reached the north coast of Spitzbergen, he found a good harbour for his ship, the *Hecla*, and left her there. The explorers had taken specially-fitted boats with them, and these they hoped to be able to haul over the ice. The summer, however, had begun to break up the floes, and in consequence the travellers had constantly to take the steel runners off the boats so that the stretches of open water could be crossed. Moreover, the floes that they did find seemed to resent such treatment, for most of them were small and bestrewn with most obstructive hummocks. Not until they had been pulling and hauling for nearly a month did they meet with large floes, and by that time the southerly drift of the ice was in full swing. However hard Parry and his men pulled, they found that the drift was as strong as they were—or stronger. After terrific labour Parry reached 82° 45', a higher latitude than any reached during the next fifty years. It was a great attempt by a man whose devotion to his duty is beyond all praise.

Before we come to the most tragic story in the history of Arctic exploration, reference must be made to the discoveries of Captain John Ross. In his first expedition to the North, Captain Ross was not successful; but in his second voyage, when he was accompanied by his nephew, James C. Ross (who afterwards gained distinction in the Antarctic), the magnetic North Pole was discovered, and the British flag fixed there in 70° 5' 17" N., and

76° 16′ 4″ W. Ross's expedition spent four consecutive winters in the Far North, discovered over two hundred miles of coastline, and returned with a bountiful crop of scientific knowledge.

We may well admire the love of adventure and the desire to make geographical and scientific discoveries which induced these constant expeditions to parts of the world that cannot possibly be called inviting. Honour was, and is, due to the men who undertook them, but to John Franklin's memory especial honour is paid, for his name is connected with both heroism and tragedy.

As a boy, Franklin, in spite of his father's opposition, determined to be a sailor. At the age of fourteen he was in the *Polyphemus* at the battle of Copenhagen, and subsequently he was present at the battle of Trafalgar. Peace, then as always, brought unemployment for sailors with it, and at the age of twenty-nine Franklin found himself unwanted in the Navy. When, however, the Admiralty decided, in 1818, to send expeditions to find the North Pole and the North-West Passage, Franklin was chosen to command the *Trent*. This ship was totally unsuited for such a task, and owing to official economy—not to say parsimony—Franklin had to return without achieving any success.

In the following year he was again sent out with orders to explore the northern coast of Arctic America, and " the trending of that coast from the mouth of the Coppermine eastwards." Not until 1822 did this expedition of discovery come to a close, after 5,550 miles had been covered by water and land.

The tale of its adventures, extraordinary as they were, is only the preface to Franklin's life as an explorer. So famous indeed was he, that when, in 1844, he returned from Tasmania, where he had been Governor for seven years, he was offered the command of an important Arctic expedition. At this time he was nearly sixty years old, but he was anxious to resume his exploratory work, and in 1845 he sailed with the *Erebus* and the *Terror* (ships that had already won their laurels under Sir James Ross in the Antarctic).

In the hope of finding the North-West Passage, so much coveted and so long concealed, Franklin was instructed to try a route by Wellington Channel, if ice did not block the way. The channel was found to be clear, and the explorers made their way up it, until they reached 77° N. Then their advance was blocked by ice, and they turned south and found winter quarters off Beechey Island. All, so far, had gone well, and when the ships were released from the ice at the end of the winter, hopes of further success must have run high. But presently a mistake was made that had fatal results—a mistake due to an error of the chart-makers.

For some time the ships sailed gaily on, important discoveries being made from day to day. Then came the fatal decision. All was open to the south. " If they had continued on their southerly course, the two ships would have reached Bering Strait. There was the navigable passage before them. But, alas! the chart-makers had drawn an isthmus (which only existed in their imagination) connecting Boothia with King William Land. They altered their course to the west, and were lost." * Soon the ships were surrounded by a dense ice-pack, and were dangerously imprisoned. In the spring of 1847 travelling parties were sent out, and one of them, under Graham Gore's command, discovered a North-West Passage, and consequently proved the connection between the Atlantic and Pacific Oceans. When the parties returned Franklin was seriously ill, and he died on 11th June, 1847.

No more beautiful epitaph has ever been written

* Markham's *The Lands of Silence* (Cambridge University Press).

than the one in Westminster Abbey, which Tennyson wrote in honour of John Franklin, his uncle-in-law :—

> " Not here ! The cold North hath thy bones, and thou,
>   Heroic sailor soul,
> Art passing on thy happier voyage now
>   Towards no earthly pole."

A terrible winter for this gallant band of explorers followed. For months and months the ice remained impenetrable, and at last the ships had to be abandoned. Even if the *Erebus* and the *Terror* could have been freed from the ice, it was more than doubtful if they would float, so battered were they by their long, slow drift. Food was both inadequate in quantity and poisonous in quality. Twenty-two officers and men died during that winter of horror; the rest were so weak from privations that, although they knew their only chance was to retreat by Back's Fish River, none of them had the strength successfully to undertake such a march.

It is useless to dwell over the sufferings of these heroic men. Captain Crozier and Captain Fitzjames took every precaution, and made all preparations that were under the circumstances possible, but the dice were too heavily loaded against them. With their two heavy boat-sledges they started on 22nd

April, 1848, to make their desperate effort. Not one
of them survived. The *Erebus* sank when the ice
released her. The *Terror* also sank, but not until
she had drifted on to the American coast and been
plundered by Eskimos. It is pitiable to think
that prompt action from England might have saved
some, at least, of these valuable lives. But at first,
although there was considerable anxiety about their
fate, no effort was made to find them. Not until
1848 were expeditions sent out in search of Franklin's
party, and neither of these was successful in finding
any traces. One of these expeditions was, however,
noteworthy, for Leopold M'Clintock, who subsequently
became so renowned as a sledge-traveller, took part
in it.

By 1850 the whole country had become thoroughly
aroused, and the Government decided to send out
strongly equipped expeditions. The *Enterprise* and
the *Investigator*, under Captains Collinson and M'Clure,
were sent out to search by way of Bering Strait ; and
four ships, under Captain Austin, were to seek for
traces of the missing party by way of Lancaster
Sound. Austin's expedition failed to find the missing
men, but it was excellently conducted and organized,
and its sledge-travellers (among whom was M'Clintock)

covered over 7,000 miles, and discovered more than
1,200 miles of new land. When Captain Austin
returned to England nothing had been heard of the
Enterprise and the *Investigator*, and after some dis-
cussion and consequent delay, it was resolved again
to send the four ships to the Arctic. Not only
Franklin's men, but also the *Enterprise* and the
Investigator had now to be searched for. It was a
case of search-parties looking for search-parties.

In their main object—that of clearing up the
mystery of Franklin and his companions—these expeditions were not successful, but in other ways they
more than justified themselves. Both Collinson in
the *Enterprise* and M'Clure in the *Investigator* succeeded in finding a North-West Passage, and much-
needed help was brought to M'Clure by the expedition
sent out partly for the purpose of aiding him and
Collinson. Further, the sledge journeys of M'Clintock and Mecham during these expeditions were un-
rivalled in result and a real triumph of organization.

Owing to the outbreak of the Crimean War in
1854, popular interest in the fate of the Franklin
expedition diminished, but Lady Franklin remained
loyal to the object to which so many years of her life
had been dedicated; and after the Government had

refused to assist her further, she decided to fit out a private expedition, of which Captain M'Clintock took command. In June, 1857, the *Fox*, a steam yacht of 177 tons, started on her voyage to Greenland, but on reaching Melville Sound, M'Clintock found it extraordinarily packed with ice. The little vessel was firmly imprisoned, and had to spend the winter in the drifting pack. During eight months she drifted southward for nearly 1,200 geographical miles, and she was not liberated from her prison until April, 1858.

After such an experience many leaders would have made for a port in which to refit, but M'Clintock was of a different temper. No sooner had the *Fox* freed herself from her perilous position than he turned her head towards the north, and once more took up the work that he had been sent out to do. And this determination to concentrate, at all costs, on the definite object in hand ultimately met with its sad reward. In June, 1859, it was proved beyond any doubt that the report of the Eskimos (which had been received in England in 1854), to the effect that they had seen the dead bodies of several of Franklin's men, was true. " All the coastline along which the retreating crews performed their fearful march must," M'Clintock wrote, " be sacred to their names alone."

Among the many feats that M'Clintock and his
men performed during this last search, were a march
round King William Island, the discovery of the one
navigable North-West Passage, and the discovery of
some 800 miles of new coastline. As far as geographical discovery was concerned, the main result of the
many expeditions sent out in search of Franklin was
that the islands to the north of North America had
been mapped out.

·In 1853 an American expedition, under Elisha
Kane, which was sent out in search of Franklin, to
the north of Smith Sound, was fruitful in geographical
discovery, and outlined what has been called the
American route to the Pole.

Interest in the Smith Sound route began to grow
in England, and was stimulated by another American
expedition, led by Charles Hall, in 1871. But although
the desire to undertake more Arctic research was
strongly felt by many Englishmen, it cannot be said
that it was encouraged in official circles. In 1872
Mr. Lowe and Mr. Goschen did receive a deputation
of Arctic enthusiasts, but were by no means encouraging in their replies. An expedition, however, under
Commander Albert Markham, set out in 1873, and
succeeded in capturing twenty-eight whales, which

were worth nearly £19,000 ; and the result of this voyage was to stimulate the idea of further Arctic enterprise.

In November, 1874, Lord Beaconsfield, who was at the time Prime Minister, announced that an Arctic expedition to encourage maritime enterprise and to explore the regions round the Pole would be sent out. Sir Clements Markham and other Arctic enthusiasts in England were delighted with this announcement, but their delight was short-lived. These enthusiasts had for years been advocating that exploratory work should be undertaken in the region round the Pole, but they did not consider that a mere rush to the Pole should be undertaken until, at any rate, work of more value to mankind had been done. The conduct of the projected expedition was taken over by the Admiralty, and great was the consternation of Sir Clements and his friends when it was announced that " the main object of the expedition was to attain the highest latitude and, if possible, to reach the North Pole."

However displeasing such an object was to these enthusiasts, they could not but rejoice at the interest shown in the expedition, and in the fact that Captain Nares was appointed to command it. At the end of

May, 1875, the ships sailed from Portsmouth, and on arriving in the Arctic regions Nares had to bear in mind his definite instructions. In short, exploratory work was to give way to an effort to reach, if possible, the Pole itself. But anxious as he was to carry out his orders, one terrible scourge stood in his way. Scurvy, that deadly disease, attacked his party during the winter, and nearly half of his men suffered from it. Under such conditions he was severely handicapped, but he decided to send out three sledge-parties—eastward, westward, and to the north. Lieutenant Pelham Aldrich was in charge of the western party, and although most of the sledge crew were weakened by scurvy, they marched over 600 miles, and succeeded in reaching 82° 48' N., a few miles farther north than Parry had reached some fifty years previously.

In 1882 an American expedition, under Lieutenant Greely, although terribly unfortunate in some respects, was successful in wresting the record for " farthest north " from the British.

We must turn aside for a moment from these efforts to get farther and farther north, to mention the exploits of that distinguished Swedish explorer, Adolf Erik Nordenskiöld. As early as 1873 Nordenskiöld began to think that the North-East Passage by the Siberian coast might, when found, prove to be of great commercial value, and after some preliminary expeditions he, in 1878, set out in the *Vega* on his great voyage, and in August the ship passed Cape Chelyuskin, the most northerly point of the Old World. By September, however, the *Vega*, when very near to the completion of her task, was so surrounded by ice that she could proceed no farther, and for ten months she was held a prisoner. Not until the following July was the *Vega* free to resume her voyage, and shortly afterwards she rounded East Cape, and saluted " the easternmost coast of Asia in honour of the completing of the North-East Passage." Nordenskiöld, both as an explorer and as a man of science, has left the world greatly in his debt, and it has been well said that " when he died, a vast amount of knowledge died with him."

Nordenskiöld's name, like Fridtjof Nansen's, is intimately connected with exploratory work in Greenland. Nansen was born in 1861, and he was only twenty-seven years of age when his devotion to discovery led him to make an expedition on lines that were as courageous as they were original. Up to this date, 1888, the recognized method employed in Polar exploratory work had been to establish a base where stores were placed, and from this base to march as far as possible in various directions. But when Nansen determined to cross Greenland from east to west, he paid no attention to recognized methods. With five companions he, in June, 1888, was taken in the *Jason* to the ice's edge on the east coast of Greenland, and there the explorers, hoping shortly to reach land, took to their boats. Some time, however, passed before they could make a landing, but eventually a suitable place was found, and then they began their great march. With no base to which they could return, the party had literally taken their lives into their hands, for failure almost certainly meant death.

Starting on 22nd August, the party, four days later, had mounted to a height of 6,000 feet, and by the middle of September had reached the summit (8,250 feet). Eventually the explorers managed to reach the Danish settlement at Godthaab, and in the following year returned to Norway. It was a fine effort, fruitful alike in geographical discovery and in meteorological results ; and, famous as Nansen's name subsequently and deservedly became, by no means his least claim to honour is derived from this great march across Greenland.

Between 1892 and 1895 the American Lieutenant Peary, using dogs for purposes of traction, made two successful marches across Greenland, and so prepared himself for the attacks on the North Pole itself—attacks which he was ultimately to bring to a successful conclusion. The date 1893 will always be renowned in the history of Arctic exploration, for during that year Nansen embarked upon his remarkable voyage in his no less remarkable ship, the *Fram*.

From careful observations and investigations Nansen was convinced that there was a continuous drift of ice from the north-east shore of Siberia across the Arctic Ocean. Hitherto, Arctic explorers had struggled hard to avoid being beset by ice. Far from following in their wake, it was Nansen's plan to get his vessel frozen in the pack, and then to drift towards the Pole.

It would be untruthful to say that his plan was encouraged by the majority of Arctic experts, but Nansen was not the man to be dissuaded from any project which, after consideration, he had taken in hand. For such a voyage an especially constructed ship was necessary, and so Mr. Colin Archer was instructed to build a vessel specially designed to resist ice-pressure. The main object of Nansen and Archer was that "she should slip like an eel out of the embraces of the ice."

Nansen calculated that the drift would take about three years, and he provisioned the *Fram* for five years. On this historic voyage Nansen was accompanied by twelve other adventurous men. Sailing from Norway in July, 1893, the Kara Sea was crossed, and early in September Cape Chelyuskin was rounded. About a fortnight later the ship was frozen in, and the great drift began. During the next months the *Fram* was given ample opportunity to prove her worth, and she seized it nobly. In October great pressure from the ice was experienced, but both then and later the ship resisted, and rose to, the pressure. During her first year in the ice the *Fram* drifted a distance of 189 miles.

During the second winter, Nansen, taking Frederik Johansen with him, and leaving Otto Sverdrup in charge of the ship, decided to leave the *Fram* and try to reach the Pole. A start was made in March, 1895, and in less than a month 86° 28' N. was reached. At that point the explorers had to turn south, and after many perilous adventures, they landed, at the end of August, on an island of the Franz-Josef group. There they decided to winter, and there they had to remain for nine long months. When at last they were able to proceed, a grave disaster was only prevented by Nansen's promptitude and courage. The explorers were on shore, when Johansen noticed that their kayaks (Eskimo canoes of light wooden framework covered with seal skins) were adrift. The loss of these boats could scarcely have meant less than death to the explorers, and Nansen immediately jumped into the icy water and swam to retrieve them. It was an action as prompt as it was heroic, and it saved the situation; but Nansen's condition, when he brought back the kayaks to land, has been described as "more dead than alive," and some time passed before he fully recovered from the results of his effort.

Some weeks later the kayaks were once more made as seaworthy as was possible under the circumstances, and Nansen and Johansen were again embarking on their adventurous voyage when, by good fortune, they were found by Frederick Jackson, the leader of the Jackson-Harmsworth Expedition, which did such good work in Franz-Josef Land. This meeting between Nansen and Jackson has been compared with the famous one between Livingstone and Stanley, and even if the latter was the more dramatic, the former was as opportune, for there is no gainsaying

that Nansen and his companion were in a most perilous position. In the meantime the drift of the *Fram*
under Sverdrup's able leadership continued, and she
did not return to Norway until August, 1896.

The results of the *Fram* expedition were exceptionally
important. "They threw," Sir Clements Markham
wrote, "new light on the whole Arctic problem.
Nansen lifted the veil, and his expedition was the
most important in modern times. It was discovered
that there was a deep-sea ocean to the north of Spitzbergen and Franz-Josef Land, extending beyond the
Pole. . . ."

In 1897 a meeting was held in the Albert Hall in
honour of Nansen, whose work, both geographically
and scientifically, more than deserved the great welcome given to him in England. In an introduction
to his *In the Northern Mists : Arctic Exploration
in Early Times*, Nansen quotes words from the old
Norse chronicle, the *King's Mirror*, that are curiously
illuminating :—

"If you wish to know what men seek in this land [the
Arctic regions], or why men journey thither in so great danger
of their lives, then it is the threefold nature of man that draws
him thither. One part of him is emulation and desire of
fame, for it is a man's nature to go where there is likelihood
of great danger, and to make himself famous thereby. An-

other part is the desire of knowledge, for it is man's nature to wish to know and see those parts of which he has heard, and to find out whether they are as it was told him or not. The third part is the desire of gain, seeing that men seek after riches in every place where they learn that profit is to be had, even though there is great danger in it."

And, indeed, it may well be admitted that the factors which have helped to make the modern world are mainly a desire for fame, a desire for knowledge, and a desire for riches; and woe betide the nation that forgets the first and second of these factors, and loses its soul in concentration upon the last of them.

II

During the years succeeding Nansen's expedition the desire to reach the North Pole itself took possession of the minds of many brave men. Bit by bit the Arctic regions had been mapped out; gradually the obstacles that maintained the Pole in its splendid isolation were being overcome. Some years were to pass before its mysteries were unveiled, but in those years there was an almost continuous effort to probe those mysteries.

Nansen had discovered beyond any doubt that the

Pole lay in an ice-covered sea, an inhospitable place enough ; but this fact did not prevent explorers from wanting actually to locate it, and in 1900 the Duke of the Abruzzi tried to reach it by way of Franz-Josef Land. Owing to a frost-bitten hand, the Duke could not take part in the main journey of his expedition, and so Captain Cagni commanded it. The Pole withstood this effort, but Cagni did succeed in reaching 86° 33′ N., and thus beat Nansen's record for " farthest north."

Previous to the Abruzzi expedition, Robert Peary had launched his first great attack upon the Pole. This expedition lasted for four years—1898 to 1902— but Peary encountered such dense packs of ice, which blocked his way to the Polar Ocean, that he failed in his main object.

Another attempt followed in 1906, and although this was not crowned with complete success, Peary made a world's record for " farthest north " by reaching 87° 6′. In this expedition he nearly lost his life, but he returned to America with the grim determination to make yet another attempt. Experience had been bought by Peary in abundance and at a great cost, and to this was added an energy that was remarkable even among Polar explorers. This third voyage to the Polar regions had, in the nature of things, to be his last. He was, when he set out upon it, fifty-three years of age, and although, after spending over twenty years in Arctic work, he had an experience that was invaluable, even experience cannot make an Arctic explorer forget that youth is also a great asset in the Polar regions.

In May, 1908, Peary published his programme, the main features of which are worthy of record. He decided to use the same ship, the *Roosevelt*, which had taken him to the north in his 1906 expedition. His route was to be by way of Smith Sound ; his winter quarters were to be at Cape Sheridan, or even nearer to the Pole if the ship could proceed farther ; he intended to use sledges and Eskimo dogs for traction ; and, lastly, he placed his confidence in Eskimos, the Arctic Highlanders, as the rank-and-file of his sledge parties.

Most careful preparations were made for this expedition, and while Peary was making them he received much practical support, but also some suggestions that were not notably helpful. For instance, one cheerful crank invited him to become a " human cannon-ball "—some sort of machine was to be taken to the North, and then, when it was pointed towards the Pole, the inventor assured Peary that it would shoot him there in no time. The explorer did not see his way to accepting such an abrupt means of transit !

When the *Roosevelt* sailed on 17th July, 1908, she had twenty-two men on board, including Peary himself, Robert Bartlett, master of the *Roosevelt*, George Wardwell, Dr. Goodsell, Professor Marvin, Donald McMillan, George Borop, and Matthew Henson, Peary's negro assistant, who had accompanied him on many expeditions.

When Peary's vast knowledge of the Polar regions is remembered, his remarks on the essentials required in an Arctic sledge journey must admittedly be valuable. " The essentials, and the only essentials," he writes, " needed in a serious Arctic sledge journey, no matter what the season, the temperature, or the duration of the journey—whether one month or six— are four : pemmican, tea, ship's biscuit, condensed milk." * And it is interesting to note that of these commodities he took 50,000 lbs. of pemmican, 10,000 lbs. of biscuit, 800 lbs. of tea, and 100 cases· of condensed milk on this expedition.

The *Roosevelt* reached Cape York, Greenland, on

* Robert Peary's *The North Pole* (Hodder and Stoughton).

1st August, and there she said a temporary good-bye to the civilized world. There also Peary met the Eskimos, whose friendship he had gained by many and continuous acts of kindness. The Eskimos are, within their limits, a lovable and loyal people; their good qualities are those of nice children, their bad qualities those of mischievous children. " I ·have made it a point," Peary says, " to be firm with them, but to rule them by love and gratitude rather than by fear and threats. An Eskimo, like an Indian, never forgets a broken promise—nor a fulfilled one." These Eskimos live on the verge of starvation for many months in the year, but if they are not troubled by questions of morality in one sense of the word, they are at any rate ready to share what they have got in the way of food, or of means to obtain it, with those who are less fortunate than themselves. Religion, as we understand it, does not enter into their scheme of things, but they pay studious attention to spirits—especially to Tornarsuk, who is the devil himself, and consequently leader of all evil spirits. One can appreciate the childlikeness of people who will rip an old garment to shreds so that the devil may be prevented from wearing it !

After leaving Cape York, Peary transferred himself

for some days to the *Erik*, his auxiliary supply steamer, so that he could collect as many Eskimos and dogs as he required. By 11th August the *Erik* reached Etah, and rejoined the *Roosevelt*. Finally, Peary selected 49 Eskimos and 246 dogs, and having transferred them to the *Roosevelt*, the explorers set out to fight their way through the 350 miles of ice-blocked water that separated Etah from Cape Sheridan. And the ice during that journey was in no gentle mood. So great were the risks that the ship might at any time be crushed, that the boats, fully equipped and provisioned, were always ready to be lowered at a moment's notice.

A terrific battle with that uncompromising opponent, the ice, followed, but not until 30th August did the struggle reach its climax. On that day the ship was " kicked about by the floes as if she had been a football," and the pressure was so terrific that Peary decided to dynamite the ice. This operation was successful in relieving the situation, but some days passed before even the greatest optimist in the ship could consider her free from danger. But on 5th September the *Roosevelt* managed to fight her way through to Cape Sheridan; and after a project to take her on to Porter Bay had been abandoned, the work of unloading her was begun, and with her lighter load Captain Bartlett proceeded to get her as near the shore as possible.

The first stage on the way to the Pole was behind the explorers, and if the next stage was shorter in distance, it was no less important a part of the whole scheme. This second stage consisted of the transportation of supplies from Cape Sheridan to Cape Columbia, ninety miles north-west of the ship. Cape Columbia is the most northerly point of Grant Land, and from there Peary had determined to make his dash over the ice to the Pole. But to move an enormous quantity of supplies over such a distance was work that needed much thought and care, for in the first place some of Peary's companions were unused to driving sledges, and, secondly, neither the weather nor the track were likely to give them much assistance.

These sledging parties on the way to Cape Columbia were soon organized, and, in addition, hunting parties were sent out, and a supply of fresh meat for the winter was obtained. " Imagine us," Peary wrote, " in our winter home on the *Roosevelt* . . . the ship held tight in her icy berth, a hundred and fifty yards from the shore, the ship and the surrounding world covered with snow, the wind creaking in the rigging, whistling and shrieking round the corners of the deck houses, the temperatures ranging from zero to sixty below, and the ice-pack in the channel outside groaning and complaining with the movement of the tides."

In these words Peary gives us an excellent picture of the explorers' winter home—a home upon which the sun never shone for many months, but which, in spite of the darkness, was a home of unceasing industry and preparation. And among the innumerable activities that took place, none was more important than the task of attending to the dogs. Early in November, Peary had become anxious about these all-important factors of his expedition. Over fifty of them were already dead, and a few days later only 160 dogs out of the 245 with which he had arrived were left. A change of diet from whale to walrus meat put an end to these appalling losses ; but Peary's anxiety until he discovered a way to prevent them can be easily imagined. For without any adequate supply of dogs he knew all too well that neither he nor any one else would ever reach the Pole.

By the end of the autumn season snow igloos had been built on the track to Cape Columbia. We have the best authority—namely, Peary's—for saying that

one of these snow-houses can be built by four good
workmen in an hour. Into this shelter the traveller
literally crawls, for the only means of entrance is
a hole at the bottom of one side, and when the last
man of the party has got in, this opening is closed up
by a block of snow already cut for the purpose.

Except for one most alarming experience, when in
a terrific gale the ice made a stupendous attempt
against the invading ship, the winter was spent rather
with anxiety about the future than with worry about
the present. No wonder that Peary speculated over
what awaited him when he started upon his great
march. After leaving Cape Columbia, over 400 miles
separated him from his goal, and these miles had to
be travelled over the ice of the Polar sea. " There
is no land," he writes, "*between Cape Columbia and
the North Pole, and no smooth and very little level ice.*"
But even ice through which the traveller must sometimes pick-axe his way is not the most serious impediment to those who would reach the Pole. The great
obstacles—the ever-present source of anxiety—are the
" leads " which constantly appear. These " leads "
are really patches of open water, varying in extent,
which the winds and tides cause in the ice's movement. For no reason that is apparent, these dangerous

obstacles suddenly block the explorer's advance, and
little can be done save to wait for them to remove
themselves. These "leads" were to be Peary's
greatest impediment in his march, and were destined
to be fatal to one valued member of his party.

The final attack on the Pole began on 15th February,
1909, when Bartlett, with a pioneer party, left the
Roosevelt, and a week later Peary started on his way.
At this time 7 members of the expedition, 19 Eskimos,
140 dogs, and 28 sledges, divided into various parties,
were engaged in the great effort to reach the Pole.
It was arranged that all of these parties should
meet Peary at Cape Columbia on the last day of
February ; and on that day Bartlett and Borop started
from the cape with advance parties. The duties of
these advance parties were as onerous as they were
important. For it was to Bartlett that Peary looked
for a trail by which the main party could travel.

On the second day's march, after Peary had left
Cape Columbia and the land behind him, he met with
his first open "lead," and a slight delay occurred. But
on the following day this "lead" was covered with young
ice, and Peary determined to cross it. "If the reader,"
he wrote, "will imagine crossing a river on a succession
of gigantic shingles, one, two, or three deep, and all

afloat and moving, he will perhaps form an idea of the uncertain surface over which we crossed this 'lead.' Such a passage is distinctly trying, as any moment may lose a sledge and its team, or plunge a member of the party into the icy water." And later on, when Borop was crossing an open crack, his dogs fell into the water, and the loss both of the dogs and the sledge with its invaluable load of provisions was only prevented by Borop's exceptional quickness and strength.

The explorers had advanced nearly 50 miles from Cape Columbia, when they were held up by a big " lead," which refused most obstinately to cover itself with ice strong enough to bear the sledges. For a week this open water delayed the expedition, and Peary had good reason to wonder if his most careful preparation and organization were once more to miss the success that they deserved. On 11th March, however, the parties managed to cross the " lead," and on the march that followed they crossed the 84th parallel.

When the explorers started on this journey, Peary did not announce how far each one of his companions was to accompany him on the march, and presently Dr. Goodsell and MacMillan, with Eskimos, sledges, and dogs, turned back. Then the main expedition consisted of 16 men, 12 sledges, and 100 dogs. On 19th March, Peary revealed the programme he intended to follow to Bartlett, Marvin, Borop, and Henson. First of all Borop was to turn back; five marches farther on Marvin was to go; and after another five marches Bartlett was to leave the Polar party, which would then consist of 6 men, 40 dogs, and 5 sledges.

Unlike most programmes, this one of Peary's was faithfully carried out. Borop returned when 85° 23' was reached, and during the next days the explorers advanced so rapidly that they succeeded in passing both Nansen's and the Duke of the Abruzzi's record for farthest north. In turn, first Bartlett and then Marvin started upon the homeward track, and Peary was left with 4 Eskimos—Egingwah, Seegloo, Ootah, and Ooqueah—Henson, 5 sledges, and 40 dogs.

Of these Eskimos, Ooqueah was the only one who had not been in any previous expedition; but all the same he was the most romantic of the party, because he was intent upon winning the rewards that would enable him to marry the girl of his choice. Glimmering before his eyes Ooqueah saw a whale-boat, a rifle, and other prizes which Peary had promised to those who went with him to the farthest point. Not for a moment was there any doubt about Ooqueah's keenness, for he was spurred on by two of the greatest incentives that any young man can have—a desire to be wealthy, and a desire to marry.

Left alone with Henson and the Eskimos, Peary still had 133 nautical miles * to travel before he reached his goal. This distance he intended to cover in five marches, and, provided that the gales would leave him in peace and not open the "leads" of water, he had every hope of carrying out his intention.

Up to this stage in the march Peary had been whipper-in, but in the last stages he led the van. And during the concluding stages it must be admitted that fortune smiled upon the travellers. True, that in this almost breathless rush for the Pole "leads" were not entirely absent, but such as were encountered did not seriously delay the marches. As, however, Peary got nearer and nearer to the Pole, the fear that the prize might at the last moment be snatched away from him by an impassable "lead" was constantly with him.

On 5th April the party reached 89° 25′ N., and were within 35 miles of the Pole. So near, indeed,

* A nautical mile is approximately 2,026 yards.

were they, that Peary writes : " By some strange shift of feeling the fear of the "leads " had fallen from me completely. I now felt that success was certain. . . ."

And his confidence was justified. On April 6, 1909, Peary, with his coloured assistant, Matthew Henson, and the four Eskimos, reached the Pole, and there the leader of this successful party wrote the following note :—

> " 90° N. Lat:, North Pole,
> *6th April* 1909.

> " I have to-day hoisted the national ensign of the United States of America at this place, which my observations indicate to be the North Pole axis of the earth, and have formally taken possession of the entire region and adjacent, for and in the name of the President of the United States of America. I leave this record and United States flag in possession.

> " ROBERT E. PEARY,
> " United States Navy."

The explorers spent thirty hours at the Pole, and then started upon the long journey back to the coast of Grant Land. By 23rd April, favoured by beautiful weather, the party had reached Cape Columbia ; so favoured, indeed, had they been that Ootah remarked on their arrival that " the devil is asleep or having trouble with his wife, or we should never have come back so easily."

On that same day Peary wrote in his diary : " I have got the North Pole out of my system after twenty-three years of effort, hard work, disappointments, hardships, privations, more or less suffering, and some risks."

The joy of success, tremendous as it was, could not but be dimmed by the news that awaited Peary on his return to the ship. For Marvin had lost his life, on the return journey, in trying to cross some young and treacherous ice, and the loss of this gallant and able man illustrates all too sadly the " some risks " of which Peary wrote—risks which all explorers in greater or less measure have to run.

As a conclusion to this chapter of adventure and determined effort, the words of that prince of explorers, Fridtjof Nansen, seem peculiarly appropriate. " From first to last," he wrote, " the history of Polar exploration is a single mighty manifestation of the power of the Unknown over the mind of man."

IV

THE MOUNTAINS OF THE MOON

THE MOUNTAINS OF THE MOON

(*Map*, p. 112.)

TWENTY-FOUR centuries ago a line of Æschylus—
" Egypt nurtured by the snow "—embodied a geographical theory which descended from Heaven
knows what early folk-wandering. Aristotle with
his ἀργυροῦν ὄρος, the Mountain of Silver from
which the Nile flowed, continued the tradition in
literature. Meantime Sabæan Arabs, trading along
the east coast of Africa, and making expeditions
to the interior, came back with stories of great
inland seas and snow mountains near them. What
they saw may have been only Kilimanjaro and
Kenia, but the popular acceptance of their reports
points to the earlier tale linking the snows with the
Nile valley. Greek and Roman travellers spread
the rumour, and presently it found its way, probably
through Marinus of Tyre, into the pages of the
geographer Ptolemy.

Ptolemy had no doubt about these snows. He called

them the Mountains of the Moon, and definitely fixed them as the source of the river of Egypt. For centuries after him the question slumbered, and men were too busied with creeds and conquests to think much of that fount of the Nile which Alexander the Great saw in his dreams. When the exploration of Equatoria began in last century the story revived, and the discovery of Kenia and Kilimanjaro seemed to have settled the matter. It was true that these mountains were a long way from the Nile watershed, but then Ptolemy had never enjoyed much of a reputation for accuracy.

Still doubt remained in some minds, and explorers kept their eyes open for snow mountains which should actually feed the Nile, since, after all, so ancient a tradition had probably some ground of fact. Speke in 1861 thought he had discovered them in the chain of volcanoes between Lake Kivu and Lake Albert Edward, but these mountains held no snow. He received a hint, however, which might have led to success, for he heard from the Arabs of Unyamwezi of a strange mountain west of Lake Victoria, seldom visible, covered with white stuff, and so high and steep that no man could ascend it. In 1864 Sir Samuel Baker was within sight of Ruwenzori, and actually

saw dim shapes looming through the haze, to which
he gave the name of " Blue Mountains."

In 1875 Stanley encamped for several days upon
the eastern slopes, but he did not realize the greatness
of the heights above him. He thought they were
something like Elgon, and he christened them Mount
Edwin Arnold (a name happily not continued) ; but
he had no thought of snow or glacier, and he disbelieved
the native stories of white stuff on the top. In 1876
Gordon's emissary, Gessi, recorded a strange appari-
tion, " like snow mountains in the sky," which his
men saw, but he seems to have considered it a halluci-
nation. Stranger still, Emin Pasha lived for ten years
on Lake Albert and never once saw the range—a fact
which may be partly explained by his bad eyesight.
Ruwenzori keeps its secret well. The mists from the
Semliki valley shroud its base, and only on the clearest
days, and for a very little time, can the traveller get
such a prospect as Mr. Grogan got on his famous walk
from the Cape to Cairo—" a purple mass, peak piled
upon peak, black-streaked with forest, scored with
ravine, and ever mounting till her castellated crags
shoot their gleaming tops far into the violet heavens."

The true discoverer was Stanley, who, in 1888,
suddenly had a vision of the range from the south-

west shore of Lake Albert. Every one remembers the famous passage :—

" While looking to the south-east and meditating upon the events of the last month, my eyes were directed by a boy to a mountain said to be covered with salt, and I saw a peculiar-shaped cloud of a most beautiful silver colour, which assumed the proportions and appearance of a vast mountain covered with snow. Following its form downward, I became struck with the deep blue-black colour of its base, and wondered if it portended another tornado ; then as the sight descended to the gap between the eastern and western plateaus I became for the first time conscious that what I gazed upon was not the image or semblance of a vast mountain, but the solid substance of a real one, with its summit covered with snow. . . . It now dawned upon me that this must be Ruwenzori, which was said to be covered with a white metal or substance believed to be rock, as reported by Kavali's two slaves."

Stanley had neither the time nor the equipment for mountain expeditions, though to the end of his life Ruwenzori remained for him a centre of romance. It was his " dear wish," as he told the Royal Geographical Society shortly before his death, that some lover of Alpine climbing would take the range in hand and explore it from top to bottom. In 1889 one of his companions, Lieutenant Stairs, made an attempt from the north-west, and reached a height of nearly 11,000 feet. Two years later Dr. Stuhlmann, a member of Emin's expedition, made a bold journey up the

Butagu valley on the west, discovered the wonderful mountain vegetation, and nearly reached the snow level. In 1895 came Mr. Scott Elliot, who was primarily a botanist, but who, in spite of bad malaria, managed to struggle as far as 13,000 feet.

Then followed troubles in Uganda, and it was not till 1900 that the work of exploration was resumed. To make the story clear, it is necessary to explain that the range runs practically north and south, and that about half-way it is cut into by two deep valleys— the Mobuku running to the east and the Butagu running to the Semliki on the west. Fort Portal at the northern end is the nearest station; and as from it the eastern side is the more accessible, it was natural that the Mobuku valley should be chosen as the best means of access. In 1900 Mr. Moore reached its head, and ascended the mountain called Kiyanja to the height of 14,900 feet. He had no sight of the range as a whole, but he believed this to be the highest peak, and put the summit at about 16,000 feet. In the same year Sir Harry Johnston followed this route. He ascended to the height of 14,828 feet on Kiyanja, and saw from the Mobuku valley a mountain to the north, which he named Duwoni. He came to the conclusion that the highest altitude of the range was not under

20,000 feet, and in this view he was followed by other travellers, like Mr. Wylde, Mr. Grogan, and Major Gibbons, none of whom, however, actually made ascents of any peak.

The first serious mountaineering expedition was made in 1905 by Mr. Douglas Freshfield and Mr. A. L. Mumm, who suffered from such appalling weather that they had to give up the attempt. Being experienced mountaineers, however, they reached some valuable conclusions. From the plains they had a clear view of the tops, and ascertained that the mountain called Kiyanja at the head of the Mobuku valley was certainly lower than a twin-peaked snow mountain beyond it to the west. They also placed the extreme height of the range at no more than 18,000 feet. Meanwhile Lieutenant Behrens, of the Anglo-German Boundary Commission, had made an elaborate triangulation, and gave to the twin tops of the highest peak altitudes of 16,625 feet and 16,549 feet —measurements, let it be noted, which were only a few hundred feet out. One other expedition, which occupied the close of the same year and the beginning of 1906, deserves mention. Mr. A. F. R. Wollaston, of a British Museum party, found an old ice-axe in a hut (probably left by Mr. Freshfield), and, with a few yards of rotten rope, set off with a companion to climb Kiyanja. He reached a height of 16,379 feet, and also climbed a peak to the north, which he believed wrongly to be Duwoni, and which now very properly bears his name. The whole performance was a brilliant adventure, and Mr. Wollaston has published the story of his travels in a delightful book.*

Such was the position when, in April, 1906, the Duke of the Abruzzi and his party left Italy to solve once and for all the riddle of the mountains. The Duke was perhaps the greatest of living mountaineers. As a rock-climber his fame has filled the Alps, and no name is more honoured at Courmayeur or the Montanvert. He had led Polar expeditions, and had made the first ascent of the Alaskan Mount St. Elias. His experience, therefore, had made him not only a climber but an organizer of mountain travel. It was to this latter accomplishment that he owed his success, for Ruwenzori was not so much a climber's as a traveller's problem. The actual mountaineering is not hard, but to travel the long miles from Entebbe to the range, to cut a path through the dense jungles of the valleys, and to carry supplies and scientific apparatus to the high glacier camps, required an organizing talent of the first order.

* _From Ruwenzori to the Congo_ (John Murray).

The Duke left no contingency unforeseen. He
took with him four celebrated Courmayeur guides,
and a staff of distinguished scientists, as well as
Cav. Vittorio Sella, the greatest of living mountain
photographers. So large was the expedition that two
hundred and fifty native porters were required to
carry stores from Entebbe to Fort Portal. It was not
a bold personal adventure, like Mr. Wollaston's, but a
carefully planned, scientific assault upon the mystery
of Ruwenzori. The Duke did not only seek to ascend
the highest peak, but to climb every summit, and map
accurately every mountain, valley, and glacier. The
story of the work has been officially written,* not
indeed by the leader himself, who had no time to spare,
but by his friend and former companion, Sir Filippo
de Filippi. It is an admirable account, clear and yet
picturesque, and it is illustrated by photographs and
panoramas which have not often been equalled in
mountaineering narratives.

The charm of the book is its strangeness. It tells
of a kind of mountaineering to which the world can
show no parallel. When Lhasa had been visited,
Ruwenzori remained, with the gorges of the Brahma-

---

* *Ruwenzori; An Account of the Expedition of H.R.H. the Duke of
the Abruzzi* (London : Constable).

putra, one of the few great geographical mysteries unveiled. Happily the unveiling has not killed the romance, for the truth is stranger than any forecast. If the Mountains of the Moon are lower than we had believed, they are far more wonderful. Here you have a range almost on the Equator, rising not from an upland, like Kilimanjaro, but from the "Albertine Depression," which is 600 or 700 feet below the average level of Uganda ; a range of which the highest peaks are 1,000 feet higher than Mont Blanc, which is draped most days of the year in mist, and accessible from the plains only by deep-cut glens choked with strange trees and flowers. The altitude would in any case give every stage of climate from torrid to arctic, but the position on the Line adds something exotic even to familiar mountain sights, draping a glacier moraine with a tangle of monstrous growths, and swelling the homely Alpine flora into portents. The freakish spirit in Nature has been let loose, and she has set snowfields and rock *arêtes* in the heart of a giant hothouse.

The Duke of the Abruzzi was faced at the start with a deplorable absence of information. Even the season when the weather was most favourable was disputed. Mr. Freshfield, following Sir Harry Johnston's advice, tried November, and found a perpetual shower-bath. Warned by this experience, the Duke selected June and July for the attempt, and was fortunate enough to get sufficient clear days to complete his task, though he was repeatedly driven into camp by violent rain. Another matter in doubt was the best means of approach to the highest snows. The obvious route was the Mobuku valley, but by this time it was pretty clear that Kiyanja, the peak at its head, was not the highest, and it was possible that there might be no way out of the valley to the higher western summits. Still, it had been the old way of travellers, and since the alternative was the Butagu valley right on the other side of the range, the Duke chose to follow the steps of his predecessors.

Just before Butiti he got his first sight of the snow, and made out that a double peak, which was certainly not Johnston's Duwoni, was clearly the loftiest. Duwoni came into view again in the lower Mobuku valley, and the sight, combined with the known locality of Kiyanja, enabled the expedition to take its bearings. Duwoni was seen through the opening of a large tributary valley, the Bujuku, which entered the Mobuku on the north side between the Portal Peaks. Now it had been clear from the lowlands that the highest

snows were to the south of Duwoni, and must consequently lie between that peak and the Mobuku valley.
The conclusion was that the Bujuku must lead to
the foot of the highest summits, while the Mobuku
could not. The discovery was the key of the whole
geography of the range. But the Duke did not at once
act upon it. He wisely decided to explore Kiyanja
first; so, thinning out his caravan and leaving his
heavier stores at the last native village, he with his
party pushed up the Mobuku torrent.

The Mobuku valley falls in stages from the glacier,
and at the foot of each stage is a cliff face and a waterfall. The soil everywhere oozes moisture, and where
an outcrop of rock or a mat of dead boughs does not
give firmer going, it is knee-deep in black mud. The
first stage is forest land—great conifers with masses
of ferns and tree-ferns below, and above a tangle of
creepers and flaming orchids. At the second terrace
you come to the fringe of Alpine life. Here is the
heath forest, of which let the narrative tell :—

" Trunks and boughs are entirely smothered in a thick
layer of mosses which hang like waving beards from every
spray, cushion and englobe every knot, curl and swell around
each twig, deform every outline and obliterate every feature,
till the trees are a mere mass of grotesque contortions, monstrous tumefactions of the discoloured leprous growth. No

leaf is to be seen save on the very topmost twigs, yet the forest is dark owing to the dense network of trunks and branches. The soil disappears altogether under innumerable dead trunks, heaped one upon another in intricate piles, covered with mosses, viscous and slippery when exposed to the air ; black, naked, and yet neither mildewed nor rotten where they have lain for years and years in deep holes. No forest can be grimmer and stranger than this. The vegetation seems primeval, of some period when forms were uncertain and provisory."

But the third terrace is stranger still. There one is out of the forest and in an Alpine meadow between sheer cliffs, with far at the head the gorge of Bujongolo and the tongue of the glacier above it. But what an Alpine meadow !—

" The ground was carpeted with a deep layer of lycopodium and springy moss, and thickly dotted with big clumps of the papery flowers, pink, yellow, and silver white, of the helichrysum or everlasting, above which rose the tall columnar stalks of the lobelia, like funeral torches, beside huge branching groups of the monster senecio. The impression produced was beyond words to describe ; the spectacle was too weird, too improbable, too unlike all familiar images, and upon the whole brooded the same grave deathly silence."

It is a commonplace to say that in savage Africa man is surrounded by a fauna still primeval ; but in these mountains the flora, too, is of an earlier world —that strange world which is embalmed in our coal

seams. Under the veil of mist, among cliffs which
lose themselves in the clouds, the traveller walks in
an unearthly landscape, with the gaunt candelabra of
the senecios, the flambeaus of the lobelias, and the
uncanny blooms of the helichryse like decorations at
some ghostly feast. The word "helichryse" calls up
ridiculous Theocritean associations, as if the sunburnt
little "creeping-gold" of Sicily were any kin to these
African marvels! Our elders were wise when they
named the range the Mountains of the Moon, for such
things might well belong to some lunar gorge of Mr.
Wells's imagination. Beyond Kiyanja the Duke found
a little lake where a fire had raged and the senecios
were charred and withered. It was a veritable Valley
of Dry Bones.

Bujongolo offered the expedition a stone-heap over-
hung by a cliff, and there the permanent camp was
fixed. Among mildews and lichens and pallid mist
and an everlasting drip of rain five weeks were passed
with this unpromising spot as their base. The first
business was to ascend Kiyanja. This gave little
trouble, for the ridge was soon gained, and an easy
arête to the south led to the chief point. The height
proved to be 15,988 feet, and the view from the summit
settled the geography of the range and confirmed the

Duke's theories. For it was now clear that the ridge at the head of the Mobuku was no part of the watershed of the chain, and that the Duwoni of Johnston was to the north, not of the Mobuku, but of the Bujuku. The highest summits stood over to the west, rising from the col at the head of the Bujuku valley. The Duke saw that they might also be reached by making a detour to the south of Kiyanja, and ascending a glen which is one of the high affluents of the Butagu, the great valley on the west side of the system.

It may be convenient here to explain the main features of the range, giving them the new names which the expedition invented, and which are now adopted by geographers. Kiyanja became Mount Baker, and its highest point is called Edward Peak after the then King of England. Due south, across the Freshfield Pass, stands Mount Luigi di Savoia, a name given by the Royal Geographical Society and not by the Duke, who wished to christen it after Joseph Thomson the traveller. Due north from Mount Baker, and separated from it by the upper Bujuku valley, is Mount Speke (the Duwoni of Johnston), with its main summit called Vittorio Emanuele. West of the gap between Baker and Speke stands the highest summit of all, Mount Stanley, with its twin peaks Margherita and Alexandra. North of Mount Speke is Mount Emin, and east of the latter is Mount Gessi. Five of the great *massifs* cluster around the Bujuku valley, while the sixth, Mount Luigi di Savoia, stands by itself at the south end of the chain.

The assault on Mount Stanley was delayed for some days by abominable weather. At last came a clear season, and the Duke with his guides crossed Fresh-field Pass and ascended the valley at the back of Mount Baker. There they spent an evening, which showed what Ruwenzori could be like when clouds are absent. They found a little lake, embosomed in flowers, under the cliffs, and looking to the west they saw the sun set in crimson and gold over the great spaces of the Congo Forest. Next day they reached the col which bears the name of Scott Elliot, and en-camped on one of the Mount Stanley glaciers at the height of 14,817 feet. At 7.30 on the following morn-ing they reached the top of the first peak, Alexandra, 16,749 feet high. A short descent and a difficult piece of step-cutting through snow cornices took them to the summit of Margherita (16,815 feet), the highest point of the range :—

" They emerged from the mist into splendid clear sunlight. At their feet lay a sea of fog. An impenetrable layer of light ashy-white cloud-drift, stretching as far as the eye could reach, was drifting rapidly north-westward. From the immense moving surface emerged two fixed points, two pure white peaks sparkling in the sun with their myriad snow crystals. These were the two extreme summits of the highest peaks. The Duke of the Abruzzi named these summits Margherita and Alexandra, ' in order that, under the auspices of these two royal ladies, the memory of the two nations may be handed down to posterity—of Italy, whose name was the first to resound on these snows in a shout of victory, and of England, which in its marvellous colonial expansion carries civilization to the slopes of these remote mountains.' It was a thrilling moment when the little tricolor flag, given by H.M. Queen Margherita of Savoy, unfurled to the wind and sun the embroidered letters of its inspiring motto, ' Ardisci e Spera.' "

The conquest of Mount Stanley was the culminating point of the expedition. After that, the topography being known, it only remained to ascend the four *massifs* of Speke, Emin, Gessi, and Luigi di Savoia. In addition, the Bujuku valley, with its tributary the Migusi, was thoroughly explored. The aim of the Duke being completeness, many of the peaks were ascended several times to verify the observations. There is an account of how from one peak in a sudden blink of fine weather the leader saw two portions of the expedition in different parts of the range moving about their allotted tasks. The result of this wise organization is that to-day the world knows every peak, glacier, and valley in Ruwenzori far more minutely than many habitable parts of the East African plateau. The expedition was not only a fine adventure, but a wonderful piece of solid and enduring scientific work. No Englishman will grudge that the honours of the pioneer fell to so brilliant a climber and so unwearied a traveller as the Duke of the Abruzzi. The Italian name has always stood high in mountaineering annals, and the Duke has long ago earned his place in that inner circle of fame which includes Mummery and Guido Rey, Moore and Zsigmondy.

The riddle of equatorial snow has been solved, and there is nothing very startling in the answer. The upper part of the mountains has no marvels to show equal to the giant groundsels and lobelias and the forests of heath on the lower slopes. The glaciers are all small, without tributaries, as in Norway ; and there are no real basins, but merely " a sort of glacier caps from which ice digitations flow down at divers points." All the same, the glacier formation is more respectable than Mr. Freshfield thought, for he saw only the small ice-stream at the head of the Mobuku, and was not aware of the much greater one from Mount Stanley which descends to the upper Bujuku valley.

The limit of perpetual snow is about 14,600 feet. Mr. Freshfield was so struck by the small size of the Mobuku torrent where it issues from the glacier, and by its clearness, that he thought it must come from some underground spring rather than from a real melting of the ice. He maintained that tropical glaciers were consumed mainly by evaporation and only in a small degree by melting. The Duke has, however, made it clear that the glaciers of Ruwenzori are subject to the same conditions as those of the Alps, and that their streams are true glacier torrents. The limpidity of the water he ascribes to their almost complete immobility, which means that there is no grinding of the detritus in their beds.

On the whole, the range offers no great scope for the energies of the mountaineer. The ice and snow work is easy, and even the huge cornices, such as are found on Margherita, are fairly safe for the climber, owing to the way in which they are propped by a forest of ice stalactites caused by the rapid melting of the snow. On the other hand, there is abundance of rock climbing of every degree of difficulty, for the mountains below the snow-line fall very sheer to the valleys. Luigi di Savoia, Emin, and Gessi are virtually rock peaks ; an isolated summit, Mount Cagni, is wholly rock; and there are fine rock faces on Mount Baker and the Edward and Savoia Peaks of Mount Stanley. I doubt, however, if Ruwenzori will ever be a centre for the rock gymnast. The weather would damp the ardour of the most earnest *habitué* of Chamonix or San Martino. A few hours of sunshine once a week are not enough in which to plan out routes up cliffs whose scale far exceeds the measure of the Alps. The Grèpon or the Dru would have long remained virgin if their crags had been for ever slimy with moisture and draped in mist, and the climber had to descend to no comfortable Montanvert, but to a clammy tent among swamps and mildews.

And yet those peaks remain almost the strangest of the world's wonders, and their ascent will always be one of the finest of human adventures. They are Mountains of the Moon rather than of this common earth. The first discoverers brought back tales which were scarcely credible—ice-peaks of Himalayan magnitude, soaring out of flame-coloured tropic jungles. For long mountaineers were consumed with curiosity as to what mysteries lay behind that veil of mist. For all they knew, equatorial snow might be difficult beyond the skill of man, and Ruwenzori the eternal and unapproachable goal of the adventurer's ambition. The truth is prosaic beside these imaginings. Any man who can afford the time and the money, who selects the right time of year, and is sound in wind and limb, can stand on the dome of Margherita.

But the experience will still be unique, for these mountains have no fellows on the globe. There is a certain kinship between the tale of the first ascent of Mount McKinley in Alaska,* and that of the Duke of the Abruzzi. That gaunt icy peak is as unlike the ordinary snow mountain as Ruwenzori. The climb began from the glacier at a height of 1,000 feet, and 19,000 feet of snow and ice had to be surmounted. The Alaskan giant and the Mountains of the Moon stand at the opposite poles of climate, but both are alike in being outside the brotherhood of mountains. They are extravagances of Nature, moulded without regard to human needs. For mountains, when all has been said, belong to the habitable world. They are barriers between the settlements of man, and from their isolation the climber looks to the vineyards and cornlands and cities of the plains. An ice-peak near the Pole and a range veiled in the steaming mists of the Line are solitudes more retired

* See Chapter VI.

and sanctuaries more inviolate. The common mountain-top lifts a man above the tumult of the lowlands, but these seem to carry him beyond the tumult of the world.

V

THE SOUTH POLE

THE SOUTH POLE

(*Map,* p. 144.)

I

THE imaginations of bold men were captured by the idea of Arctic exploration for centuries before the Antarctic was even thought of as a field for discovery. The Arctic regions have a history dating back to the days of King Alfred; the Antarctic can make no such boast as this, and it is true to say that attention was first drawn to the Far South by the map-makers.

Much praise is due to the early map-makers; but as regards the Far South it must be admitted that they indulged in considerable guesswork. Ortelius, for instance, in his map of the world which was published in Antwerp in 1570, had the temerity to draw the coast of " Terra Australis nondum cognita " round the world as far north, in two places, as the Tropic of Capricorn.

Hakluyt did, in 1599, omit the Southern continent

from his celebrated map of the world, an abstinence on his part that deserves to be mentioned. But fictions, in spite of Hakluyt, continued to appear in later maps; and if they did nothing else, they were at least useful in directing the thoughts of navigators towards the Antarctic.

Accident rather than design was, however, responsible for the first discoveries in the South. In 1520 Magellan found the strait which is known by his name, and during the sixteenth century what discoveries were made in the direction of the South were due to contrary winds. Owing to gales, Sir Francis Drake, in 1578, reached in latitude 56° S. "the uttermost part of the land towards the South Pole," and so, sadly against his will, made discoveries. And it was owing to what has happily been called "a discovery-causing gale" that some Dutch ships, which had set out in 1598 for the exciting but scarcely laudable purpose of plundering the coasts of Chile and Peru, were scattered in all directions. One of these ships, a mere baby of 18 tons, was driven to 64° S., and there her captain, Dirk Gerritsz, sighted "high land with mountains covered with snow, like the land of Norway."

If proof of the universal ignorance of the South

at the beginning of the seventeenth century is needed, we have the expedition of Pedro Fernandez de Quiros. Quiros was commissioned by the King of Spain, Philip III., to undertake a voyage for the purpose of annexing the South Polar continent; and after this annexation had been completed, he was commanded to convert the inhabitants to the true faith. It was an ambitious programme, and it was far indeed from being carried out. In fact, the result of the expedition was almost comical. Quiros discovered the largest island of the New Hebrides, and in the belief that it was part of the Southern continent, he not only annexed it, but also the South Pole itself, to the Crown of Spain! This expedition must be considered the first Antarctic expedition, but there is no denying that its results were more ludicrous than encouraging.

Little progress was made during the seventeenth century in adding to the world's knowledge of the South, but in one way and another the map-makers received severe buffets. Towards the end of that century and the beginning of the next, some ships reached 62° S. and 63° S., and encountering great icebergs, gained knowledge that tended to disperse the idea of a huge continent, from which men could reap wealth and live in comfort while reaping it. In spite, however, of this waning belief in a fertile and populous Southern continent, several voyages were undertaken to look for it ; but it is to be noted that the men who made these adventurous journeys were not in the least interested in exploration for exploration's sake. The reason why they made these expeditions was mainly because they hoped to enrich themselves. Not until the latter half of the eighteenth century was there any change in what may be called the spirit of exploration ; and then, in 1764, the English Government issued instructions to Commodore Byron which clearly showed that the importance of discovery, for discovery's sake alone, was beginning to be realized.

Science had been making progress, and the desire really to know, and no longer to guess at, the extent and nature of the world perceptibly increased. Scientists, engaged solely on scientific work, accompanied both the expeditions of Marion and Kerguelen, and when Captain James Cook sailed in 1772 from Deptford, on what was the first British Antarctic expedition, he was also accompanied by scientists.

The name of James Cook will always be given a place of honour among explorers, for, quite apart from the discoveries that he made, he set an example of courage in facing dangers and difficulties that can never be forgotten. He and all the earlier navigators, we must remember, had to undertake their voyages in ships that were totally unfit to encounter ice. And when this fact is realized, we are compelled to admire the pertinacity with which they carried out their work, and to recognize that the results of their efforts were, under the circumstances, magnificent.

It has been well said that James Cook defined the Antarctic region and that James Ross discovered it; and, indeed, it would be difficult to overestimate the importance either of Cook's voyages or of those subsequently undertaken by Ross.

January 17, 1773, was a red-letter day in the annals of exploration, for during its forenoon Cook crossed the Antarctic Circle for the first time. Icebergs and loose pack-ice were then surrounding him, but he pushed on until he sighted closely packed ice. In his opinion he might possibly have pushed his way through this ice, but in such a ship as the *Resolution* (462 tons) he did not consider himself justified in making so dangerous an experiment. The latitude that he reached was 71° 10′ S., longitude 106° 54′ W.

Cook's expedition returned to Portsmouth in July,

1775, and then the value of his voyage was recognized. He had made the circuit of the Southern ocean in a high latitude, and had for ever crushed the idea of a fertile and fruitful Southern continent. If land lay beyond the Antarctic Circle, Cook thought that it must consist of " countries condemned to everlasting rigidity by Nature, never to yield to the warmth of the sun, for whose wild and desolate aspect I find no words." Cook, in short, had revealed the limits of the habitable globe, and his accounts of what he had encountered in the Far South did not encourage men, who were anxious to find land in which fortunes could quickly be made, to think longingly of the Antarctic.

After Cook's return no serious attempt at geographical discoveries in the South was made until the Russian Government, in 1819, sent an expedition, under Captain Bellingshausen, to the Southern seas. Bellingshausen's ambition was to rival Cook's feat of making the circuit of the Southern ocean in high latitude, and he achieved it. He was also the first explorer definitely to discover land within the Antarctic Circle.

Two or three years later James Weddell, whose real business was sealing, reached a latitude of 74° 15' S., more than three degrees to the south of Cook's farthest point ; and for nearly twenty years Weddell's record remained intact.

During the first half of the nineteenth century the Southern seas became the scene of extensive sealing industries, and however much we may regret the wholesale slaughter that took place, we have to confess that some of these sealers made important geographical discoveries. Both Captain John Biscoe and Captain John Balleny were engaged in the Antarctic sealing trade, but they were fortunate enough to be employed by the firm of Enderby. Charles Enderby instructed his captains not to neglect geographical discovery, and his instructions were faithfully carried out. To the enterprise of Enderby, and to the courage and perseverance of his captains, we owe the discovery of Graham Land, Enderby Land, Kempe Island, and Sabrina Land.

A French expedition under Captain D'Urville, and an American one under Captain Wilkes, followed in 1840. D'Urville, who encountered so many icebergs that he felt as if he was "in the narrow streets of a city of giants," sighted land in latitude 66° S., longitude 140° E., and named this coast Adélie Land. Wilkes also claimed to have discovered land ; but of his claims one of our greatest explorers has written : " Had he been more circumspect in his reports of land, all would have agreed that his voyage was a fine performance."

Two or three years before D'Urville and Wilkes set out upon their voyages, Colonel Sabine, at a meeting of the British Association, read a paper on the subject of terrestrial magnetism, and the result was that Polar exploration received a great incentive. By this time the importance of terrestrial magnetism in regard to the navigation of ships was admitted, and the Government was petitioned to send a naval expedition for the purpose of increasing our knowledge of this science in the South. A favourable reply was received from Lord Melbourne, and in 1839 Sir James Ross was appointed to command an expedition whose object was rather magnetic research than geographical discovery. Two old bomb vessels, the *Erebus* (370 tons) and the *Terror* (340 tons), were selected by Ross, and when their bows had been strengthened he had at his disposal the first vessels that could be navigated among the Southern pack-ice. A detailed account of Ross's achievements cannot be given, but of them Captain Scott wrote : " The high mountain ranges and the coastline of Victoria Land were laid down with comparative accuracy from Cape North in latitude 71 to Wood Bay in latitude 74, and their extension was indicated less definitely to McMurdo Bay in latitude 77½. . . . Few things could have looked more hopeless than an attack upon that ice-bound region which lay within the Antarctic Circle ; yet out of this desolate prospect Ross wrested an open sea, a vast mountain region, a smoking volcano (Erebus), and a hundred problems of interest to the geographer." *

The highest latitude reached by Ross was 78° 10′ S., and he described the huge wall of ice which he sighted there and named the Great Barrier, as a " mighty and wonderful object, far beyond anything we could have thought of or conceived." This Barrier was in later years found to be 400 miles wide, and of even greater length.

Slowly, very slowly, the Far South was being compelled to reveal some of its secrets, but in spite of the interest and enthusiasm caused by Ross's discoveries, many years passed, after his return to England in 1843, before further steps were taken to make geographical discoveries in the Antarctic.

But during this period, in which geographical enterprise languished, scientific research was being carried

* *The Voyage of the " Discovery "* (John Murray), page 16.

on. A great desire to increase the knowledge of the science of oceanography had sprung up, and as a practical outcome of the labours of scientists and inventors, the *Challenger* expedition, excellently equipped for scientific research, set out under the command of Captain Nares in January 1873. This expedition was in itself most important, but it is not belittling it to say that part of its value in the history of Antarctic exploration lies in the fact that it stimulated interest in the Far South, and this interest gradually increased until the wish to solve the mysteries of the South Polar regions became dominant in the minds of many men in England and Germany. In 1885 the British Association appointed an Antarctic Committee, and some two years later this Committee reported in favour of further exploration.

Great difficulties, chiefly financial, had, however, to be faced by the supporters of this expedition, and a shrewd blow was received when the Board of Trade refused to recommend a grant of money because there were no trade returns from the Antarctic regions!—a reply that might produce a derisive smile from the most zealous of economists. For the moment the idea of Antarctic exploration had received a decided setback. But determined men were working to conquer

the practical difficulties; and none more determined
than Sir Clements Markham, who was elected President
of the Royal Geographical Society in May 1893.
No sooner was it generally known that a real effort
was being made in England to make further discoveries
in Antarctica—as it was by this time called—than
several other countries were stimulated at various
dates to send out expeditions. Borchgrevink, a Norwegian, De Gerlache, a Belgian, Otto Nordenskiöld, a
Swede, and Charcot, a Frenchman, led expeditions,
all of which did valuable work in the South.

II

In November, 1893, a meeting of the Royal Geographical Society was held, and the duties of the projected British expedition were stated. The first duty
was "to determine the nature and extent of the
Antarctic continent;" the fifth was "to obtain as
complete a series as possible of magnetic and meteorological observations." Such an expedition was
intended both to encourage maritime enterprise and
to add to the world's knowledge. From the outset
the promoters had decided that their expedition
should be under naval control, but the Government

could not be persuaded to take charge of it. The Admiralty, however, assisted both with the loan of instruments and by granting leave to officers and men on full pay.

Innumerable obstacles continued to hamper the promoters on every side, but they were slowly removed, and at last the ship was launched at Dundee in March, 1901, and christened the *Discovery*.

Sir Clements Markham, fourteen years before, had, in his own mind, selected the fittest commander if an expedition to the South ever became practicable. The name of this commander was Robert Falcon Scott, and after much opposition had been overcome —opposition which Sir Clements described as " harder to force a way through than the most impenetrable of ice-packs "—Scott's appointment was confirmed. A great attack upon the Antarctic regions was about to be made, but it is worthy of record that in the instructions issued to Captain Scott no mention of the South Pole as an objective was made.

By July the labour of preparation for the expedition was almost finished, and on August 5, 1901, the *Discovery* was visited by King Edward VII. and Queen Alexandra, and then started on her adventurous voyage. We can easily understand Scott's anxiety

to be up and away, for he had no Polar experience
to help and guide him, and his desire to justify the
confidence placed in him must have been intense.

In the *Discovery*, in addition to Scott himself, were
several men whose names were destined to become
famous in the history of Polar exploration. Ernest
H. Shackleton was a second-lieutenant; Ernest A.
Wilson was described as surgeon, artist, and vertebrate
zoologist; Edgar Evans was a petty officer; Frank
Wild and Thomas Crean were A.B.'s; William Lashley
was a stoker. Surely the nucleus of a goodly company.

Lyttelton, New Zealand, had been chosen for the
headquarters of the expedition in the South, and the
Discovery arrived there on 30th November. She
stayed for three weeks to re-fit and take in provisions,
and then started upon the next stage of her eventful
journey. The Antarctic Circle was crossed on 3rd
January, and soon afterwards the pack was on all
sides of the ship; but she behaved splendidly, and
Scott was delighted with the way she forced herself
through the ice.

Scott's original intention had been that the *Discovery*
should not winter in the Antarctic, but that, having
landed a party of men, she should return northward
before the ice made such a journey impossible. A

hut had been provided for this party, but in February a spot was found in McMurdo Sound in which it was thought that the ship would pass the winter in safety. Consequently Scott decided to use the *Discovery* as his headquarters, and to utilize the hut for other purposes.

The task of erecting the huts (in addition to the main hut there were two smaller ones for magnetic work) was difficult, but it was eventually accomplished, and the party began to settle down to spend the approaching winter. Before, however, the winter set in, Scott, knowing how ignorant he and his companions were of sledging, was anxious to gain as much experience as possible. And the result of the sledging expeditions that were made only showed how urgently this experience was needed. " Even at this time [early in March]," Scott wrote, "I was conscious how much there was to be learnt, and felt that we must buy our experience through many a discomfort; and on looking back I am only astonished that we bought that experience so cheaply, for clearly there were the elements of catastrophe as well as of discomfort in the disorganized condition in which our sledge-parties left the ship." *

When the *Discovery* was brought into McMurdo

* *The Voyage of the " Discovery,"* page 170.

Sound there was good reason to suppose that she would soon be frozen in. But weeks passed before the sea became frozen, and until the ship was firmly fixed in the ice there was always a chance that she might be driven away by a gale and be unable to return. This uncertainty hampered operations for some time, and it was not until the last days of March, 1902, that the ship was satisfactorily frozen in.

The sun departed at the end of April, and during the long winter that followed the party of explorers had much to occupy them and to discuss. Scott had taken dogs with him for sledging purposes, but although he knew that they must increase his radius of action, he always detested the idea of using them because of the suffering that must necessarily be caused. But the question of using dogs was only one of the many problems in connection with sledging that was debated during that Antarctic winter.

In judging the journeys that followed in the spring, it is to be remembered that as far as the Antarctic regions are concerned they were pioneer efforts, and also that the conditions of Antarctic sledging differ considerably from those of the Arctic. In these journeys Scott and his companions were taught lessons that were afterwards of the greatest value to other explorers as well as to themselves—lessons that nothing except experience could teach.

The journey that Scott, with Wilson, Shackleton, and several dogs, began on 2nd November with the object of pushing as far south as possible, was accompanied at the outset by a supporting party; but this party turned back by the 15th, and Scott, Wilson, and Shackleton had immediate cause to know how strenuous a task they had before them. The dogs were already causing anxiety, and were quite unable to do the work expected from them. Relay work, which meant that each mile had to be travelled three times, became the order of the day, and in consequence the advance towards the South was greatly hindered. Soon afterwards the men themselves began to suffer from blistered noses, cracked lips, and painful eyes; but on the 21st Scott took a meridian altitude, and found the latitude to be 80° 1′.

In spite of all discomforts and anxieties, Scott was in a happy mood that night when he wrote: " All our charts of the Antarctic regions show a plain white circle beyond the eightieth parallel. . . . It has always been our ambition to get inside that white space, and now we are there the space can no longer be a blank; this compensates for a lot of trouble."

As the advance laboriously continued, the condition
of the dogs, to Scott's poignant sorrow, went from
bad to worse, and by 21st December the question of
turning back had to be considered. At this time
additional anxiety was caused by Shackleton, who
was showing symptoms of scurvy; but Christmas
Day was in sight, and as on that festival the travellers
had decided to have a really satisfying meal, they
resolved to push on farther.

Their meal on Christmas Day put new life into the
party; but they realized all too acutely that their food
supplies were so inadequate that, if they were to
continue the advance they must be prepared to face
the risk of famine. There were, however, strong
incentives to urge them on their way. Each day took
them farther and farther into regions hitherto un-
trodden by the feet of men. Who can blame them
for taking the risks that were involved in their determination to continue the march ?

But on 27th December, Wilson, whose industry in
sketching and determination not to give in were
beyond praise, was suffering so severely from snow-
blindness that he had to march blindfold ; and at last ·
the decision to turn back had to be made. Observations taken at their last camp showed that they had

reached between 82° 16′ and 82° 17′ S.—a finer record than Scott anticipated, after he had realized that the dogs were unable to fulfill the hopes placed in them.

The return march was a prolonged period of suspense. By January 9, 1903, only four out of the nineteen dogs which had started on the journey were alive, and on the 15th the last of them had to be killed. "I think," Scott wrote, "we could all have wept." Even more serious was the fact that at this time Shackleton became seriously ill.

A grim struggle followed, for although Shackleton showed unending courage he was suffering severely from scurvy, and Scott and Wilson, who were themselves attacked in a lesser degree by this disease, often had cause to wonder whether this return journey was not beyond their powers. It was with feelings of profound thankfulness that, at the beginning of February, Scott and his companions reached the ship. For ninety-three days they had been on the march, and during that time they had travelled 960 statute miles.

When the explorers reached their goal they found that the relief ship, the *Morning*, had arrived, and Shackleton returned in her ; but the *Discovery*, after being so reluctant to freeze firmly into the ice, refused entirely to thaw out, and consequently Scott and

most of his original party spent a second winter in the
Antarctic. During this additional year Scott, with
Edgar Evans and Lashley as his companions, made a
wonderful western journey, in which adventures
enough to last ordinary men for a lifetime were almost
part of the daily routine.

Not until February, 1904, was the *Discovery* freed
from the ice, and on 10th September she reached
Spithead after an absence from England of over three
years. In those years a crop of most useful information had been gathered, and many geographical discoveries had been made. Among the latter were
King Edward Land, Ross Island, and the Victoria
Mountains, and—most important of all—the great ice-
cap on which the South Pole is situated.

Not for some years yet was the South Pole to reveal
its secret, but Scott's first expedition may truthfully
be said to have shown the way towards that revela-
tion. In the years to come Amundsen frankly admitted
how carefully he and his companions studied the
accounts of Scott's and Shackleton's expeditions.

III

After Scott's return from his first visit to the
Antarctic no further attempt was immediately made

to visit the Far South. But that great explorer, Ernest Shackleton, had seen enough of the South to be gripped by the desire to solve more of its problems, and in the *Geographical Journal* of March, 1907, he stated the programme of a proposed expedition. In this programme Shackleton said : " I do not intend to sacrifice the scientific utility of the expedition to a mere record-breaking journey, but say frankly, all the same, that one of my great efforts will be to reach the southern geographical Pole."

The financial difficulties that seemed to be inseparable from Polar expeditions followed, but they were ultimately removed, and on July 30, 1907, the *Nimrod* sailed for New Zealand.

Bearing in mind the failure of the dogs in Scott's expedition, Shackleton decided to use Manchurian ponies as his principal means of traction. The utmost care was taken in preparing the equipment and in choosing the staff to accompany the expedition. Shackleton intended to land a shore party, and among this party were Frank Wild and Ernest Joyce (who had been with Scott), Douglas Mawson, Lieutenant J. B. Adams, Dr. E. Marshall, Raymond Priestley, and G. E. Marston.

Before leaving England, Shackleton decided, if

possible, to establish his winter quarters on King
Edward VII. Land in preference to Scott's old quarters
at Hut Point in McMurdo Sound ; but he was unable
to carry out this plan, and ultimately he landed close
to Cape Royds on the east coast of Ross Island. On
February 22, 1908, his ship, the *Nimrod*, started upon
her journey to New Zealand.

The winter quarters that had necessarily to be chosen
were separated from Hut Point by some 20 miles of
frozen ice, and Shackleton was greatly disappointed
that he was prevented from landing on King Edward
VII. Land, where he would not only have broken fresh
ground, but would also have been considerably nearer
to the Pole. In the light of subsequent events it is of
interest to note that Shackleton, in his search for winter
quarters off the Barrier, looked with eagerness upon a
bay which he named " The Bay of Whales," but
owing to the conditions of the ice he thought it necessary to leave this spot as quickly as possible. In
another respect this expedition met with poor fortune—namely, in the loss of ponies. When the party
settled down to spend the winter only four ponies
were still alive, and it is no cause for wonder that they
were watched with the closest attention. And as a
Manchurian pony has been endowed with more than

his fair share of original sin, he requires a very great deal of watching.

Before the winter set in, an attempt was made to reach the top of Mount Erebus, and this attempt met with a success that acted as a tonic both to those who took part in it and to those who had remained in winter quarters. As soon as mid-winter day had passed, Shackleton began to make arrangements for the sledging work that had to be done in the approaching spring. Depots had to be laid in the direction of the South Pole, which was over 880 statute miles distant from Cape Royds.

These preparations went on apace, and with a view to starting on the Southern march from the nearest possible point to the Pole, stores, etc., were transferred to Hut Point, and depots were also laid to help the travellers on their way. Adams, Marshall, and Wild were chosen to accompany Shackleton in this determined effort to reach the South Pole, and on 29th October they set out with the four ponies and the four sledges. By 3rd November they had left the sea-ice and were on the Barrier; but instead of finding a better surface they found it increasingly difficult. At the outset, however, the ponies did splendid work, though one of them, on 9th November, nearly disappeared into "a great fathomless chasm." At the time the travellers were in a nest of crevasses, and Adams's pony suddenly went down a crack. Fortunately, with help from Wild and Shackleton, the pony and the sledge were saved from falling into this abyss; but it was an alarming incident, for, as all the cooking gear and biscuits and a large portion of the oil were on this sledge, the loss of it would have been an irretrievable disaster to the Southern journey.

The 26th November was a day to be remembered by Shackleton and his companions, for at night they found that they had reached latitude 82° 18′ S., and so had passed Scott's "farthest south." On 1st December, latitude 83° 16′ S. was reached, but by this time three of the ponies had been killed, and only one was left. A few days later this last pony disappeared down a crevasse, and nearly took Wild and the sledge with him. Serious as the loss of this gallant pony was, there was great cause for thankfulness that Wild and the sledge had almost miraculously been saved. Had the sledge gone, only two sleeping bags would have been left for the four men, and the equipment would have been so short that the explorers could scarcely have got back to winter quarters.

Presently the travellers left the Barrier and attacked

the great Beardmore Glacier which was between them and the plateau. On 9th December, 340 geographical miles lay between them and the Pole, and progress was painfully slow, for the surface consisted mainly of rotten ice through which their feet continually broke. A week later they had travelled over nearly 100 miles of crevassed ice, and had risen 6,000 feet ; but the plateau which they so eagerly longed to reach still lay ahead of them. " Never," Shackleton wrote, " do I expect to meet anything more tantalizing than the plateau." Appalling surfaces, to walk on which Wild described as like walking over the glass roof of a station, continued after the plateau had been reached, and before Christmas arrived it was obvious, if the advance was to be continued, that absolute hunger, amounting almost to starvation, stared the explorers in the face.

On the evening of New Year's Day, 1909, the Pole was only 172½ miles distant, but the men's strength was nearly exhausted. The thermometer remained obstinately below zero, and on 6th January there were over 50 degrees of frost, with a blizzard and drift. A last dash onwards followed, and on 9th January Shackleton and his party reached 88° 23′ S., and left the Union Jack flying on the plateau. The attempt to reach the Pole had failed; but it was a gallant attempt, and the homeward marches that followed show clearly enough that to have advanced farther was beyond the powers of the men. Indeed, the return journey was a terrible experience—a grim struggle against starvation; and to add to the misery of it, dysentery—owing, in Shackleton's opinion, to eating diseased pony's meat—attacked each member of the party. All that was possible had been done, and had not the wind been behind the explorers during one of their acutest periods of suffering, it is improbable that they would ever have reached their winter quarters.

While Shackleton was making his great march, a party, consisting of David, Mawson, and Mackay, had set out, with a view to determining the position of the south magnetic Pole. In this they were successful, the mean position of the magnetic Pole being marked down by Mawson as in latitude 72° 25′ S., longitude 155° 16′. This was a great triumph for the explorers, and, needless to say, it was not gained without many perilous adventures and narrow escapes.

In March, 1909, the *Nimrod* returned safely to Lyttelton, New Zealand, where Shackleton and his men met with the warmest of welcomes. Once again the South Pole had resisted the attempt to locate it, but the time was drawing near for its mysteries to be disclosed.

III

When, on September 13, 1909, Captain Scott published his plans for a British Antarctic expedition in the following year, Roald Amundsen was not thinking about the Far South. The *Fram*, it is true, was being prepared for a third voyage, but the Arctic was again to be her destination. Then, during the September of 1909 came the news that Peary had reached the North Pole. One of the great secrets of the world had been revealed; but another was still undiscovered, and Amundsen's thoughts were promptly turned from the Arctic to the Antarctic.

For various reasons Amundsen did not announce his change of plans, and when the *Fram* sailed in August, 1910, only a very few people knew where she was bound for. Not until the ship left Madeira did Amundsen announce his destination to the men who were accompanying him, and they received the news with joy.

In two or three respects Amundsen's expedition differed considerably from Scott's new expedition.

Amundsen, for instance, relied on dogs for his motive power; Scott relied on ponies. Then, again, Amundsen decided to make his winter headquarters off the Bay of Whales, which was a degree farther south than McMurdo Sound, where Scott wintered. Scott was to take the Beardmore Glacier as his route to the South Pole; Amundsen's plan, when he set out for the Pole, was to leave Scott's route alone and push straight south from his starting-place. "Our starting-point lay 350 geographical miles," Amundsen wrote, "from Scott's winter quarters in McMurdo Sound, so there could be no question of encroaching upon his sphere of action." Lastly, it must be mentioned that the Norwegians were as at home on ski as they were on their feet, while most of Scott's men were at their best only moderate performers upon ski.

All went well with the *Fram* on her voyage to the South. She crossed the Antarctic Circle on January 2, 1911, and twelve days later she was in the Bay of Whales. In landing on the Great Barrier, Amundsen knew that he was taking a considerable amount of risk, for there was no certainty that it was not afloat where he landed on it from the Bay of Whales. In Amundsen's opinion, however, the Barrier there rests

" upon a good solid foundation, probably in the form of small islands, skerries, or shoals." *

And indeed the Barrier treated him well. The landing was performed with supreme ease, and enough seals were found to relieve any possible anxiety as to the supply of fresh meat. Penguins, those delightful birds which provide both humour and food for visitors to Antarctica, were not plentiful, and those that were seen were chiefly of the Adélie species.

" Framheim," the hut in which the South Pole party were to live during the winter, was soon erected, and Amundsen found infinite satisfaction in the number of dogs which were safely landed. So far from losing dogs on the voyage, he had started with 97 and finished with 116, a most welcome addition.

The *Fram*, leaving eight men to winter on shore, was due to sail in the middle of February upon an oceanographical cruise, but before leaving she received some unexpected visitors. On 4th February, Captain Scott's ship, the *Terra Nova*, with the party which had vainly hoped to land on King Edward VII. Land, came into the Bay of Whales.

The news that Amundsen was safely established reached Scott on 22nd February, and he could not fail

---

* Amundsen's *The South Pole* (John Murray), Vol. I., page 49.

to be impressed by it. " One thing only," he wrote characteristically, " fixes itself definitely in my mind. The proper, as well as the wiser, course for us is to proceed exactly as though this had not happened; to go forward and do our best for the honour of the country without fear or panic. There is no doubt that Amundsen's plan is a very serious menace to ours. He has a shorter distance to the Pole by 60 miles. I never thought he could have got so many dogs safely to the ice. But above and beyond all, he can start his journey early in the season—an impossible condition with ponies." * Words that, in the light of future events, are more than ordinarily significant.

Before the winter set in Amundsen determined to deposit food, etc., on the way to the Pole, and on 10th February he set out on his first journey with three men, three sledges, and eighteen dogs.

This first trip upon the Barrier was full of exciting possibilities. Amundsen was without knowledge of the ground over which he had to travel, and he did not know whether the dogs would respond to the demands made upon them, or if his outfit would stand the severe test to which it was to be put. This was essen-

* *The Voyages of Captain Scott* (John Murray), page 259.

tially a trial trip, and the travellers were naturally anxious that it should be successful. Eighty degrees South was reached, and in every respect save one Amundsen was satisfied with his journey. The only fly in his ointment was that time had been wasted in preparations before the party was ready to start in the mornings. But it was only a small fly, and Amundsen knew that with thought it could easily be removed. The dogs had responded so splendidly to the calls made upon them, that perhaps the most important question of all had been satisfactorily answered.

More depot-laying expeditions followed, and before the winter closed around the explorers, they had placed three tons of supplies at depots in latitudes 80°, 81°, and 82° S. Amundsen and his men could, therefore, settle down for their period of waiting with justifiable hopes that the great spring march to the Pole would end in triumph.

The winter was spent in paying attention to the minutest details of equipment, and the inhabitants of " Framheim " were kept gloriously busy and contented. But with the coming of spring Amundsen began to be impatient to be up and away on his great journey. Temperatures, however, remained very low

—somewhere in the neighbourhood of − 60° F.—and until they ceased "to grovel in the depths," no start, could be made.

With the beginning of September the temperatures began to improve, and Amundsen was determined to start as soon as he possibly could, arguing that he could turn round and come back if he found that he had started too soon. So on 8th September he did set out, and soon discovered that the dogs could not endure the intense cold. On the 11th the temperature was − 67.9° F.; on the following day it was − 61.6° F., with a breeze dead against the travellers. On reaching the 80° S. depot, Amundsen deposited more stores, and then returned to "Framheim."

More than a month passed before the South Pole party was able to make another start, and it is of interest to note that, whereas Amundsen ultimately got off on 19th October, Scott was unable to start before 1st November.

The South Pole party which set out from "Framheim" consisted of Amundsen, Hanssen, Wisting, Hassel, and Bjaaland, and they were accompanied by fifty-two dogs drawing four sledges. As an illustration of the dangers that lay between the explorers and the Pole, it is enough to say that on the first day's journey a terrible disaster was only avoided by a few inches. In the thick weather they had steered too far to the east, and almost fell into what Amundsen describes as "a yawning black abyss, large enough to have swallowed us all, and a little more."

On the 21st Bjaaland's sledge sank down a crevasse, and had to be unloaded before it could be brought again to the surface. Wisting, with the Alpine rope fastened round him, went down and unloaded the sledge, and when he came up again and was asked if he was not glad to be out of such a position, he replied, "It was nice and warm down there."

It is true that such events are far from unusual in the lives of Polar explorers, but Wisting's answer is worth quoting, because it is typical of the cheerful spirit shown by Amundsen's companions during the whole of the journey. In temperament they were admirably suited for the task that they had undertaken.

With a view to landmarks on the return journey, Amundsen, rightly leaving nothing more to chance than he could help, decided to build snow-beacons. The first beacon was built in 80° 23' S., and altogether 150 beacons were erected, six feet in height.

Up to 82° S. the course had already been travelled

by depot-laying parties, but when, on 6th November, they left 82° S. behind them, their journey was absolutely into the unknown. At this time they were marching about 23 miles daily, and at this rate they advanced a degree in three days.

On reaching 83° S., the explorers deposited provisions for five men and twelve dogs for four days, and depots were subsequently made at 84° S., and 85° S. It was from the latter depot that they decided to make what may, without exaggeration, be called their dash for the Pole. From their camp at 85° S., the distance to the Pole and back was 683 miles. After consideration Amundsen determined to take forward provisions, etc., for sixty days on the sledges, and depot the rest of the supplies and outfit.

A weary ascent to the plateau lay before the explorers, and they started upon it on 17th November. Three days later they had reached the plateau, but although they were happy enough in having accomplished a long and dangerous climb, their first camp on the plateau was not one of happy memory.

Grim work had to be done. Amundsen arrived on the plateau with forty-two dogs, but twenty-four of them had to be killed when the plateau was reached. It was a sacrifice that had to be made if the success of the expedition was to be considered; but no one can read Amundsen's account of it without recognizing how bitterly he and his companions regretted the necessity.

This camp, not without reason, was called " The Butcher's Shop," and as both the men and dogs required rest before setting out on the final stages of their march, it had been decided to remain there for two days. The eighteen remaining dogs were divided into three teams, with six dogs in each team, and one sledge was left behind.

But owing to the weather the explorers could not leave this hated " Butcher's Shop " until 25th November, and when they did set out again a blizzard was blowing. So tired, however, were they of waiting in such an inhospitable and gruesome spot, that all of them were eager to quit it—whatever the conditions of the weather might be.

Fog subsequently impeded the party, and again and again Amundsen blessed the assistance that they received from ski. " I am not," he wrote, " giving too much credit to our excellent ski when I say that they not only played a very important part, but possibly the most important of all, on our journey to the South Pole. Many a time we traversed stretches of surface so cleft and disturbed that it would have been an impossibility to get over them on foot." *

The 7th December was a great day for the expedition, because during it they passed Shackleton's "farthest south," 88° 23' S. They proceeded for another two miles, and then determined to make their last depot. So important to them was this depot that they not only marked it at right angles to their course, but also by snow beacons at every two miles to the south.

As the explorers approached the Pole, Amundsen, very naturally, was beset by nervousness. "Would he be there first?" was a question that kept on recurring in his mind. There was no cause to worry. Blessed by fine weather, he and his companions reached the South Pole on December 14, 1911, and the five of them together planted the pole from which the Norwegian flag flew. "Thus we plant thee, beloved flag, at the South Pole, and give to the plain on which it lies the name of King Haakon VII.'s Plateau."

On this day Scott was still struggling on his great march to the same destination, which he reached in the third week of January.

* *The South Pole*, Vol. II., page 89.

The calculations that Amundsen carried out at the South Pole gave its latitude as 89° 56′ S.

Amundsen had won the race, and with his victory had revealed one of the great secrets of the world. His success had been gained by strenuous labour, great courage, and infinite care. And if Britons connect Scott's name inseparably with the South Pole, and honour it as that of one of their heroes, they do not for a moment grudge Amundsen the honour due to him as one of the greatest explorers of all time. For Amundsen was the first to discover the South Pole, and no one wishes, or is likely, to forget it.

The Norwegians reached the Pole with seventeen dogs, one of which had to be killed there, and they travelled back with two sledges, a team of eight dogs in each sledge. On his return journey Amundsen was fortunate enough to meet with favourable winds and weather, and the explorers arrived at " Framheim " on January 25, 1912, having travelled 1,860 miles in ninety-nine days. It was a glorious achievement, a great victory over conditions that are scarcely conceivable to any one unacquainted with the Antarctic or Arctic regions.

IV

To pass from Amundsen's expedition to Scott's last expedition is to turn from one splendid exploit to another. Scott, as every one knows, was beaten in the actual race for the South Pole. But he and his friends reached their goal, and the tale of their struggle against misfortune after reaching it is one of the finest and most pathetic in the world.

When Scott's intentions to lead another Antarctic expedition were known, no less than eight thousand applicants volunteered to go with him, and among this enormous number were several men whose names will for ever find a place in the history of Polar exploration.

When the *Terra Nova* sailed from Lyttelton, New Zealand, for the Antarctic regions, on November 29, 1910, she carried both ponies and dogs. Three motor-sledges, one of which was lost in landing, were also taken, and Scott, with his intense dislike for the cruelty inseparably connected with the use of animals for motive power, hoped that these sledges would do much to save the ponies and dogs. Owing to engine trouble these hopes were not realized, but in connection with them Sir Clements Markham has written: "Captain Scott was quite on the right tack, and, with more experience, his idea of Polar motors will hereafter be made feasible, a consummation which was very dear to his heart." *

The *Terra Nova* was by no means as fortunate as the *Discovery* in making her way to the Antarctic. At the beginning of December she encountered a prolonged and terrific storm, and subsequently she had to fight her passage through some 370 miles of ice. Not until January 3, 1911, did she reach the Barrier, five miles east of Cape Crozier. Here Scott had hoped to make his winter quarters, but owing to the swell no landing could be made, and on the following day he decided to land at Cape Evans, 14 miles north of the *Discovery's* winter quarters. Strenuous work followed, and in a few days everything necessary had been landed from the ship, the house was soon built, and the explorers were ready to start laying depots in preparation for the march to the Pole.

On his first depot-laying journey Scott was accompanied by eleven men, eight ponies, and twenty-six dogs. He was more than a little doubtful about the dogs, but thought his ponies were bound to be a success.

* *The Lands of Silence* (John Murray), page 490.

"They work," he wrote, "with such extraordinary steadiness. . . . The great drawback is the ease with which they sink into soft snow—they struggle pluckily, but it is trying to watch them."

This depot-laying party reached latitude 79° 29' S., and there left over a ton of stores; consequently the name of One Ton Camp was bestowed upon it. On the return journey disasters happened that seriously affected the success of the expedition, for six out of the eight ponies were lost. "Everything out of joint with the loss of our ponies, but mercifully with all the party alive and well," is Scott's comment on this grave misfortune. Ten ponies still remained.

During the winter Wilson, Bowers, and Cherry-Garrard started on June 27, 1911, upon their famous journey to Cape Crozier to visit the Emperor penguin rookery, and they did not return to Cape Evans until 1st August. During these weeks they had to fight against appallingly low temperatures. When, for instance, they started from Cape Evans, their three sleeping-bags weighed 52 lbs., but owing to the ice that had collected upon them these three bags weighed 118 lbs. when the travellers returned. Scott considered that no praise was too high for men who would face such weather during the Polar winter.

With the beginning of August preparations for the great march went on apace, but it was not until 1st November that a' start could be made from Cape Evans. Night-marching was decided upon, and the order of marching was at first settled by the speed of the ponies, for some of them were slow, some fairly fast, and some were "fliers." The motors, with E. R. Evans, Day, Lashley, and Hooper with them, had already started, and the dogs, under the control of Meares and Demetri, were to follow behind the last detachment of men and ponies. Very soon, however, the motor-party were in trouble, and this party had to abandon their machines and push on as a man-hauling party.

By 15th November Scott reached One Ton Camp, and fears about the ponies began to take shape. At Camp 19 the explorers were within 150 miles of the Beardmore Glacier, but some of the ponies were beginning to fail, and at the next camp the first of them ("the gallant Jehu") had to be shot. From this camp it was arranged that Day and Hooper should turn back.

At Camp 22 the Middle Barrier depot was made in latitude 81° 35', and then for some days the march was impeded by extraordinarily foul weather. Scott's desire was to take the ponies as far as the entrance to the Beardmore Glacier; but although, on 29th November, at Camp 5, they were only 70 miles from what he calls his "pony-goal," some of the willing animals were very tired.

At Camp 29 six ponies were still left out of the ten which had started, but although the chances of getting through successfully to the glacier were good, the weather still remained as obstructive as possible.

On 5th December a terrific fall of snow added to the anxieties of the explorers, who found themselves within 12 miles of the glacier, but hopelessly held up by such a violent and unexpected storm. It was natural enough for Scott to be anxious, for on 7th December the food that he had hoped only to use after the glacier was reached had to be begun on. Two days later, however, by marching under terrible conditions, the entrance to the glacier was gained, and then at Camp 31, which was called Shambles Camp, the last of the ponies were killed.

On 9th December, Wilson wrote: "Nobby [Wilson's special pony] had all my biscuits last night and this morning, and by the time we camped I was just ravenously hungry. Thank God the horses are now all done with, and we begin the heavy work ourselves."

At Camp 32 the Lower Glacier depot was built, and soon afterwards Meares and Demetri, with the dogs, turned back for home. At this time the parties were made up of—

Sledge 1. Scott, Wilson, Oates, and P. O. Evans.

Sledge 2. E. Evans, Atkinson, Wright, and Lashley.

Sledge 3. Bowers, Cherry-Garrard, Crean, and Keohane.

But by 21st December, in latitude 85° S., Scott had to send back four of these men, and Atkinson, Wright, Cherry-Garrard, and Keohane returned. The Upper Glacier depot was made, and the returning men took back a letter from Scott in which he wrote : "So here we are practically on the summit, and up to date in the provision line. We ought to get through."

On New Year's Day, 1912, the party were within 170 miles of the Pole. Three Degree depot was made. Then in latitude 87° 32' S., Scott was compelled to send back E. R. Evans, Crean, and Lashley. When all of the men were so anxious to go on it was hard to have to part with any of them ; but questions of food made it absolutely necessary that some of the party should return.

The ages of the five men who marched on to the

Pole were : Scott, forty-three years old ; Wilson, thirty-nine ; P. O. Evans, thirty-seven ; Oates, thirty-two ; and Bowers, twenty-eight. Again and again Scott expressed his admiration of his four companions : Wilson, " never wavering from start to finish " ; Evans, " a giant worker " ; Bowers, " a marvel—he is thoroughly enjoying himself " ; Oates, " goes hard all the time."

With such men Scott felt confident, in spite of terrible surfaces, of reaching the Pole. But as he approached it, fears that Amundsen had already arrived were constantly besetting him ; and on 16th January, when within a few miles of the longed-for goal, there was no longer any doubt that the Norwegian party had won the race. Sledge and ski tracks and the traces of dogs were all too evident.

Faced by such a grievous blow, not one of Scott's party could sleep that night, but on the day following they marched on some 14 miles and reached the Pole. "The Pole," Scott wrote, "yes, but under very different circumstances from those expected."

It is impossible to conceive a greater blow, and when it is remembered that Scott and his four companions were already fatigued—if not completely exhausted— by their tremendous labours, it is easy to realize how heavily the disappointment hung on their minds. Nevertheless they had set out to reach the Pole, and they had reached it. All honour is due to them ; and the fact that Amundsen had preceded them in no way diminished the glory of their achievement.

The altitude of the Pole, as estimated by Scott, is about 9,500 feet. A cairn was built, and the Union Jack hoisted. And then on Thursday, 18th January, they turned their backs upon their goal, and began the long march that separated them from Cape Evans. Anxiety about food began at once—not until Three Degree depot was reached could it be lessened ; and very soon anxiety at Evans's condition was added to the danger of the scarcity of food.

On Wednesday, 31st January, the weary travellers reached the Three Degree depot, but by this time Evans had dislodged two finger-nails, and his general condition was very bad. Their next objective was the Upper Glacier depot, and on Monday night, 5th February, they were within from 25 to 30 miles of it ; but so critical had the health of Evans become that Scott was desperately eager to get off the plateau. "Things," he wrote, "may mend for him [Evans] on the glacier, and his wounds get some respite under warmer conditions."

On the evening of 7th February they reached the Upper Glacier depot, and then, after turning aside to collect geological specimens (which proved to be most valuable), they met with terrible surfaces and weather. On 14th February, with 30 miles still to go before the Lower Glacier depot was reached, Scott's anxiety about the condition of the party was acute. Indeed, poor Evans had almost reached the limit of human endurance, and during the night of 17th February he became unconscious, and died quietly at 12.30 a.m.

It was a terrible experience for men, already supremely fatigued both in mind and body, to meet, and it was a sorrowful party which, on Sunday afternoon, arrived at Shambles Camp. There horse meat in plenty awaited them, and this gave them the renewal of strength that was sadly needed. For the moment the prospects of the explorers looked a little more hopeful, but from this point of their march they began to suffer from a lack of oil. When, at length, they succeeded in arriving at the Middle Barrier depot, on 2nd March, they found so little oil that it was scarcely enough, however economically used, to carry them on to the next depot, which was 71 miles distant. Another irretrievable disaster was the fact that Oates's feet were very badly frost-bitten. On 4th March, Scott

wrote : " I don't know what I should do if Wilson
and Bowers weren't so determinedly cheerful over
things." And in all truth the position had become
desperate. On the 7th, when still 16 miles short of
Mount Hooper depot, Oates, though wonderfully
brave, was in terrible pain. During the next day
they arrived at Mount Hooper, but the shortage of
oil was not relieved.

Over 70 miles separated the exhausted travellers
from One Ton Camp, and they struggled onwards
with death staring them ever nearer and nearer in the
face. With no helping wind, and bad surfaces, they
could not advance more than six miles a day, and on
the night of the 11th, Scott reckoned up the situation
in these words : " We have seven days' food, and
should be about 55 miles from One Ton Camp to-night ;
$6 \times 7 = 42$, leaving us 13 miles short of our distance,
even if things get no worse."

Unhappily, instead of any improvement in the
situation, misfortunes became more and more plentiful.
It was obvious that Oates was near the end, and on
the morning of the 15th or 16th, when the blizzard
was blowing, he walked out of the tent. " I am just
going outside, and may be some time," were the last
words he spoke to his companions in distress. " We

knew," said Scott, who still continued to write his
journal, "that poor Oates was walking to his death
. . . it was the act of a brave man and an English
gentleman."

Oates sacrificed himself in the hope of helping the
others, and no brave man ever performed a braver act.
But his sacrifice was of no avail. Fortune had de-
clared too strong a hand against the explorers for
them to be able to resist it.

By midday on 18th March, Scott, Wilson, and
Bowers had struggled on to within 21 miles of One
Ton depot, and during the afternoon of the following
day they managed to advance another 10 miles. And
then they made what was destined to be their last
camp. The men themselves were in a pitiable condition, and blizzard following blizzard, they were
utterly unable to march a step farther.

On 29th March, Scott wrote: "Since the 21st we
have had a continuous gale from W.S.W. and S.W.
We had fuel to make two cups of tea apiece, and bare
food for two days on the 20th. Every day we have
been ready to start for our depot, *eleven miles* away,
but outside the door of the tent it remains a scene of
whirling drift. . . . We shall stick it out to the end,
but we are getting weaker, of course, and the end

cannot be far. It seems a pity, but I do not think I can write more." And then follows those pathetic words : " Last entry. For God's sake, look after our people."

It was not until 30th October that Atkinson, on whom the leadership of the expedition had fallen, was able to take out a search party. And nearly a fortnight later the bodies of these three friends and explorers were found.

No more fitting words could be found with which to conclude this chapter of great deeds than those which were left in the metal cylinder on the grave of these heroes :—

" November 12, 1912, latitude 79° 50' S. This cross and cairn are erected over the bodies of Captain Scott, C.V.O., R.N. ; Doctor E. A. Wilson, M.B., B.C. (Cantab.) ; and Lieutenant H. R. Bowers, Royal Indian Marine. A slight token to perpetuate their successful and gallant attempt to reach the Pole. This they did on January 17, 1912, after the Norwegian expedition had already done so. Inclement weather, with lack of fuel, was the cause of their death. Also to commemorate their two gallant comrades, Captain L. E. G. Oates, of the Inniskilling

Dragoons, who walked to his death in a blizzard to save his comrades, about 18 miles south of this position; also of Seaman Edgar Evans, who died at the foot of the Beardmore Glacier.

"The Lord gave and the Lord taketh away; blessed be the name of the Lord."

VI

MOUNT McKINLEY

MOUNT McKINLEY

(*Map*, p. 184.)

THE ascent of Ruwenzori unriddled the mystery of equatorial snows. There now remained the question of great peaks in the extreme North, where the mountaineering problems must obviously be very different from those found at a similar altitude in the temperate zones. Something had been done to solve the problem by the ascent of Mount St. Elias, in Alaska, on July 31, 1897. But Mount St. Elias was only just over 18,000 feet, and it was peculiarly accessible, for it lies close to the coast, on the borders of British and American territory. The eyes of explorers began to turn towards Mount McKinley, the highest peak in North America, which reached a height of 20,300 feet. Its latitude was 63° N., and so within 250 miles of the Arctic Circle. The nearest salt water, Cook Inlet, was 140 miles from the southern face as the crow flies. It was therefore almost unreachable, lying as it did in the midst of an unexplored wilderness and surrounded by a mighty glacier system.

On the south these glaciers were drained by the Susitna River, with its tributaries the Yentna and the Chulitna, and on its northern face by the affluents of the Yukon. If the traveller attempted to reach it in summer he might find a difficult waterway up to the beginning of the glaciers, but then he had thirty miles of ice to cross before he reached the base, and over these he must transport everything on his back. In winter the journey might be made by dogs, but winter in those latitudes was scarcely the time to travel. Moreover, Mount McKinley, unlike the other great peaks in the world, rose from a low elevation. In the case of the South American and Himalayan peaks climbing does not begin until an altitude of at least 10,000 feet has been reached, and their line of perpetual snow is very high. It is possible, for example, to cover the 22,860 feet of Aconcagua without ever touching snow. But in Mount McKinley the snow-line was not much more than 2,500 feet, and there was something like 15,000 feet of climbing. Again, its position so far north did not permit the snows to melt properly in the summer, or to grow hard and pack. Its snowfall was so great that the snow never got into the condition which eases the path of the mountaineer. Finally—and this applied especially to a winter journey—it was situated in a land of desperate storms. The severest weather conditions ever recorded by the American Meteorological Bureau occurred at Mount Washington, which is only 6,000 feet above the sea, where the temperature was 40 degrees below zero and the wind 180 miles an hour. What might the climber expect 20,000 feet up in the sky, with nothing between him and the North Pole ?

The attempt on Mount McKinley, therefore, was not a thing to be lightly undertaken. It meant a journey to the remote Alaskan coast, and then some 200 miles through difficult and little known country before even the base was reached. What the climbing would be like no one could tell. The obvious route, as the map will show, was the Susitna River, by which, indeed, its first explorer, a young Princeton graduate called Dickey, had approached it in 1896. It was he who christened it Mount McKinley. He fell into an argument with another prospector who was a rabid champion of free silver, and after many weary days' dispute retaliated by naming the mountain after the champion of the gold standard. In 1903 an expedition, led by the too famous Dr. Cook, reached the base from the north, but failed to do any climbing. Then, in 1906, began the explorations of Professor Parker and

Mr. Belmore Browne, who were destined six years later to be the conquerors of the peak.

I

The 1906 expedition may be roughly sketched, for, though it was a failure, it at least taught its leaders what routes were not possible. They started with pack-horses and a motor-boat, with the intention of trying the north-western face. They ascended the Yentna River, which enters the Susitna from the west, but found it impossible to cross the southern flanks of the Alaskan range. They then turned up the south side of the range, and reached the glacier out of which the Tokositna River flows. By this time their transport was in a precarious condition, and their horses could go no farther. They were within view of Mount McKinley, and saw not only the impossibility of the southern face, but the extraordinary difficulties of approaching even its base from that direction. They accordingly returned to the coast, where Dr. Cook left them, announcing that he intended to make one final desperate attempt on the mountain.

Presently Professor Parker and Mr. Belmore Browne

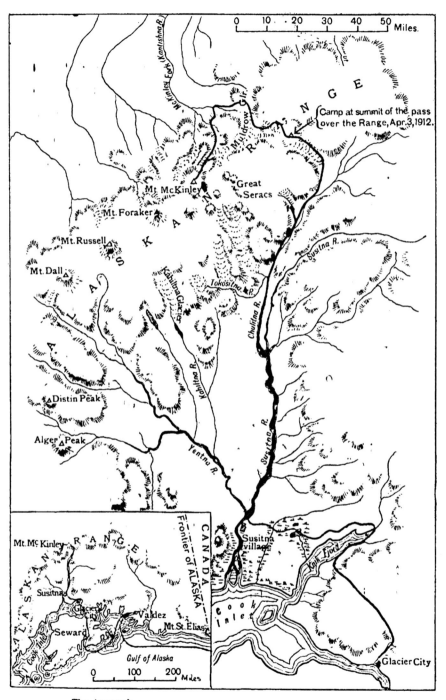

The Approach.

Mount McKinley.

heard, to their surprise, the rumour that Dr. Cook had succeeded. Knowing that the feat was impossible in so short a time, they disbelieved the tale, and stated their views publicly in New York. Then appeared Dr. Cook's notorious book; but before it was published he had departed for the Arctic regions. Geographical circles in America were torn with the controversy. A committee of the Explorers' Club investigated the question, but Dr. Cook refused to give evidence. Professor Parker and Mr. Belmore Browne were meantime busy with their own plans for another attempt.

The 1910 expedition was again directed to the southern face. Their reasons were that for most of the journey to that face a water route was possible, and that if they failed there they believed they would be able to go on to the southern North-East ridge, which, from what they had heard and seen, they believed to be the most promising avenue of attack. They also wished to duplicate the photographs which Dr. Cook had published, and so prove or disprove his *bona fides*. Also, the northern side of the great mountain had been already fairly well mapped, but nothing had been done on the south side.

The notion of a pack train was discarded, and all

their energies were directed towards designing the right kind of boat in which to ascend the Susitna and its tributary the Chulitna till they reached the glaciers. The party consisted of eight, including a young man from Seattle, Mr. Merl La Voy, who was exceptionally fitted by Providence for the work of a pioneer. The present writer had many dealings with Mr. La Voy during the Great War, and can confidently say that he never met any one more intrepid, audacious, and resourceful.

It was a summer-time expedition, and the party left Susitna station on the 26th May. The ascent of the two rivers was difficult and exciting enough, but they reached without misadventure the foot of the Tokositna tributary, where they established their base camp. This camp was thirty-seven and a half miles from Mount McKinley, and a few miles away was the terminal moraine of a great glacier, which they hoped would give them a roadway to the mountain. Up that glacier they would have to carry all their belongings on their backs. In Mr. Belmore Browne's narrative there is an interesting passage describing the process by which men are hardened to wilderness work.

" The day's work consisted in travelling through

brush, soft sand, swamps, and glacier streams for about ten hours. With the exception of one or two men, who put a biscuit in their pockets, we took no food with us. The day's work was in no way difficult, for we carried (during the preliminary reconnaissance) no loads ; our condition from the *civilized standpoint* was splendid ; we were well-fed, sun-browned, and fairly hard—and yet we all came into camp *thoroughly tired out*. Two months after our adventures on Mount McKinley's ice flanks we came down through the same stretch of country. The snow, however, had melted, leaving dense thickets through which we had to chop our way ; mosquitoes hung in clouds, and four of us . . . were carrying packs running from 95 to 120 lbs. From the civilized standpoint *we were not well-fed* and we did not look well—our eyes and cheeks were sunken and our bodies were worn down to bone and sinew ; and yet we came into camp as fresh and happy as children, and after a bite to eat and a smoke we could have gone on cheerfully."

It was no light task carrying an outfit of 1,200 lbs. over the thirty-seven and a half miles of glacier, a distance which by the actual route used was much farther. Most of the weight was in pemmican and alcohol for the stoves. The pemmican consisted of pulverized raw meat, mixed with sugar, raisins, currants, and tallow. Their principal drink was tea. On 11th June they had their last wood fire, and after that there was only the stove. The days were spent in sheer hard navvy labour, trudging along on snow-shoes under heavy packs, and trotting back for others. They had various misadventures. Frequent blizzards of wind and snow compelled them to shut up their tent fast at night, with the result that on one occasion they were nearly asphyxiated.

On 27th June they reached the head of the main glacier, beyond which, through a narrow gorge, a secondary glacier descended from the mountains, Another glacier came down on their right, and here they achieved an interesting piece of detective work. At the top of it they saw some peaks which recalled an illustration in Dr. Cook's book. The illustration purported to be the summit of Mount McKinley, and showed on the left a rock shoulder which Dr. Cook described as a cliff of 8,000 feet. It was really a faked picture of the small peaks at the head of this glacier, miles and miles from the main mountain, and the cliff of 8,000 feet turned out only to rise 300 feet above the floor, and to be only 5,300 feet above sea-level. One legend at any rate had been dispelled for ever.

Now began the patient relaying of provisions up the great gorge. It was desperately hard manual labour, their faces were burnt black by the glare of the sun, and every now and then there would be a slip into a crevasse, which only the highest good fortune saved from being a tragedy. After thirty-six days of hard travelling, they were at last within two miles of the base of the southern cliffs of Mount McKinley. They found themselves in a great ice basin, hemmed in by colossal precipices down which avalanches thundered. Before them rose the mountain, 15,000 feet of rock and ice. Their glasses showed them that the South-West ridge became utterly unclimbable after an altitude of about 15,000 feet. The southern North-East ridge looked more promising, and to this they turned their attention. In that Northern summer there was no dark. " The advance and retreat of the night shadows went on with scarcely a pause, and sometimes we would be uncertain whether the Alpine glow on the big mountain's icy crest was the light of the rising or the setting sun." They had now a short spell of rest from their toil ; and as the mind of man on such occasions turns to food, they invented out of their scanty larder a new pudding. Here is the recipe.

"First soak three broken hard-tack in snow-water until they are soft. Add 60 raisins and pemmican the size of 4½ eggs. Stir slowly but energetically until the mess is thoroughly amalgamated. Boil slowly over an alcohol stove, add three tablespoonfuls of granulated sugar, and serve in a granite-ware cup."

But between them and the North-East ridge lay a gigantic *serac*. For a day and a half they lay storm-bound under it, and then, on the morning of 11th July, tried to cut their way up the ice wall. It proved most difficult and dangerous work, and presently, owing to the diminishing provisions, they realized it was impossible. Again and again they attempted it, for only that way was there a road to the North-East ridges. But at last they had to give it up as hopeless, and turn their attention to the South-West *arête*.

This, too, proved too hard for them. They laboured on under constant ice-falls and avalanches, and reached a height of 10,300 feet, where they had perforce to halt. During these days they saw some marvellous mountain scenery. "The whole of the great cliffs of the box-cañon appeared at first glance to be on fire. Unnumbered thousands of tons of soft snow were avalanching from the southern flanks of Mount

McKinley on to the glacier floor 5,000 feet below. The snow fell so far that it was broken into heavy clouds that rolled downward like heavy waves. The force of the rolling mass was terrific, and as it struck the blue-green glacier mail it threw a great snow cloud that raced like a live thing for 500 feet; whirling in the wind the avalanche had caused, the white wall swept across the valley, and almost before we were aware of it we were struggling and choking in a blinding and stinging cloud of ice dust."

They began their retreat, and their return to greenery and summer out of a hyperborean hell was like a man's recovery from a dangerous illness. Though the expedition failed, they were a merry party, for though every man was sunken-eyed and lean and hatchet-faced, he was in the pink of condition. It was nothing to them to carry a load of 120 lbs., which would have broken their backs in the first days. The party included men of diverse temperaments and multifarious attainments, and Mr. La Voy observed, "It is an education to travel with a bunch like ours; if anything should happen you can listen to a whole dictionary." In the end they came to their cache on the Chulitna, and they emptied it as children empty their Christmas stockings. "We were actually ravenous," says Mr. Belmore

Browne, "and as jars of chow-chow, cans of maple-syrup, and tins of meat appeared we hugged them in our arms and danced delirious dances on the sand! One of the great truths of life that one learns to understand in the North is that it is well worth while to go without the things one wants, for the greater the sacrifice the greater the reward when the wish is consummated. I have eaten with all manner of hungry men, from the sun-browned riders of the sage to the bidarka-men of the Aleutians, and I have feasted joyously on ' seal-liver,' ' seagull-omelets,' and ' caribou spinach '; but never have I seen men eat more, or better food ! "

II

As soon as the explorers returned to civilization they began to plan a third attempt. It was clear to them that the western and southern faces of the mountain were impracticable, and that their best chance was on the North-East ridge. This, however, could not be approached from the south; so it became their object to get in on the north side. Their explorations in 1910 had proved the difficulties of a summer trip, for loads had to be transported on men's backs over many miles of glacier. They therefore decided to make a winter expedition of it and to use Alaskan dog teams. The best route seemed to be up the Susitna and Chulitna rivers, and they hoped somewhere near the head of the Chulitna to find a pass in the Alaskan range which would take them round the north face of Mount McKinley.

In October, 1911, Mr. La Voy began to relay supplies up the Chulitna, the plan being for him to join Professor Parker and Mr. Belmore Browne at Susitna in February of 1912. As Cook Inlet is choked by ice during winter the travellers had to leave the steamer at Seward, and make a long and difficult overland journey by way of Glacier City and the Knik fjord to the Susitna River. There they found Mr. La Voy with the dog teams. He reported that he had taken the bulk of the outfit to a cache on the Chulitna, several miles beyond the mouth of the Tokositna.

The journey up the Susitna, which was now a flat snow trail, went easily and pleasantly. When they reached the cache they found to their disgust that a wolverine, which is the arch-fiend of those northern wildernesses, had managed to break in, though it was placed for greater security on a platform of logs among the trees. The brute had destroyed a good deal of the dog-feed and bacon, and a new and expensive camera of Mr. La Voy's, which had been swung on the top of a 30-foot pole. The wolverine had climbed the pole, cut off the corners of the leather case, and gnawed its way into the camera!

From the cache began a long system of relays, for it was impossible to carry all the equipment in one journey. There was now no trail, and a road had to be " broken " before each stage. The route lay up the Chulitna, and the travellers hoped to find some large stream coming down on their left which would indicate a gap in the Alaskan range. Any such gap would, of course, be filled with glaciers, the water from which must form a river. On the whole, winter travelling compared favourably with summer. The men used snow-shoes to break the trail, and after equipment had been transported for five miles, returned on the empty sleds for new loads. Winter had not killed all signs of wild life, though hunting was difficult, and the snow was dotted with the tracks of innumerable wild things. Even a finch was heard singing. Camping was perfectly comfortable, and in a tent with the stove lit and beds of green spruce prepared, the nights were warm and peaceful.

At last, as the trees began to thin, they came to a

point where the valley split and a great cañon turned north towards the range. Travel now became rougher, for the broad level flats gave way to snow-covered rapids and big drifts. As they advanced up the gorge a glacier was seen winding down from the centre of the mountains. One night Mr. Belmore Browne had an accident which might have proved serious. He went out to shoot an owl for food, and as the ejector of his little rifle had been removed the cartridge came back on his eye and just missed his right eyeball. It gave him an eerie feeling to see the friendly dogs lapping up the bloodstained snow. Shortly after he made a reconnaissance of twenty-five miles ahead, and found the glacier they had seen from afar off running like a great white road into the hills. The route seemed possible, but there were ugly ice precipices at the head which suggested that the crossing of the pass might not be easy.

A second reconnaissance took him to the head of the glacier. At first no crossing could be discerned, but suddenly at the head of the right-hand basin the mountains broke away and he saw a smooth snowfield leading to the crest. He climbed to the top of it, and at first saw nothing but a sheer precipice. At length, however, he discovered on the right a gentle snow slope leading down into a great snow cup, and realized that the pass could be crossed.

On 3rd April the main camp was pushed up to a height of 6,000 feet. Then came a delay from a blizzard, which confined the explorers for twenty-four hours to their tents. It was bitterly cold, and everything, including the alarm clock, froze stiff. They managed, however, to get a little fire with an empty pemmican case, and, with the stove, had a sort of party in the tent—men, dogs, and everything. The party was, however, unceremoniously broken up by one of the dogs backing into the stove, and filling the tent with a cloud of smoke from singed hair.

Next morning they crossed the divide, partly shooting and partly lowering their belongings over the 1,000-feet drop into the hollow. They were no sooner across when another blizzard arrived, and they were storm-bound for thirty-six hours. But their spirits were high. For the time they were done with uphill climbs, and they saw that by crossing a low pass at the head of another glacier they could reach the great Muldrow Glacier, which had been known to the world since 1902. This glacier would take them into the very heart of the mountain.

Without much difficulty they crossed the pass, and,

descending to the Muldrow moraine, they realized with joy that they were on the northern side of the Alaskan range. It was now nearly the middle of April, and they found themselves in the kind of country that hunters dream of. There was a chance of fresh meat, and, to men who had been seventeen days on the ice, the hope of a change in their menu and the sight of vegetation were an intoxication. Mr. Belmore Browne went out one morning, and fell in with a herd of white sheep (*Ovis Dalli*). He secured three, and that night the camp feasted. " In cold weather," he writes, " one has a craving for fat, and in the wilderness one is less particular about the way meat is cooked. Our desire for fat was so intense that we tried eating the raw meat, and finding it good beyond words, we ate freely of the fresh mutton. I can easily understand now why savage tribes make a practice of eating uncooked flesh." The white sheep was not the only game. There was a special variety of caribou ; there was the Alaskan moose ; there was an occasional grizzly; and there were quantities of ptarmigan. The travellers showed the most sportsmanlike spirit in refraining from killing females or immature beasts.

From the Muldrow Glacier they turned westward and struck the McKinley fork of the Kantishna River, which flows to the Yukon. Presently they were in timber country, and realized that they had crossed the Alaskan range "from wood to wood," and incidentally had added two new glacier systems to the map. After snow and ice and pemmican they had greenery and fresh meat, and, as they worked their way to the lowlands, the first flush of spring. Above all, they had the North-East ridges (of which there were three) above them to offer an apparently possible route to the summit. They saw a glacier running between the central and northern North-East ridges which they decided would be their road. Mr. Belmore Browne went out to prospect, and, climbing the head of a valley, found himself looking down upon the upper Muldrow Glacier, which he now realized was split in two by the central North-East ridge. He saw also that the northern branch of it gave a road to the very base of the central peak.

A base camp was established on 24th April, and four days later began the chief reconnaissance. They took with them a dog team, and, for equipment, their mountain tent, instruments, alcohol lamps, and provisions of pemmican, chocolate, hard-tack, sugar, and raisins. The total outfit weighed about 600 lbs. They started at night, when the snow was in better condition, and found the northern branch of the Muldrow, which they called the McKinley Glacier, rising in steps like a huge staircase. Camp was pitched at the base of a *serac* between two great cliffs of solid blue ice.

On 3rd May they reached the top of the *serac* at an altitude of 8,500 feet, after a very difficult journey. Mr. La Voy, who was leading, fell into a crevasse, and the strain on the rope pulled Mr. Belmore Browne to the very edge. Mr. La Voy, however, stuck on a ledge of ice, which eased the strain ; without that ledge it may well be that the whole expedition would have ended in tragedy. Bit by bit they fought their way to the head of the glacier, suffering severely from the glare of the sun, though the temperature was only one degree above freezing. They had now attained an altitude of 11,000 feet, and saw a low col on the mountain ridge, where they decided to make a high camp. This would be about 12,000 feet high, which would leave them between 3,000 and 5,000 more feet to climb before they reached the basin between the north and south peaks. It was now time to send the dogs home ; so, after caching their equipment, they started back for the base camp, which they reached on the evening of 8th May.

Some pleasant days were spent at the base camp. When they left it the countryside had still been in the grip of winter, but now everywhere there were grass and flowers and running streams. So far they had managed well. They had crossed the Alaskan range early enough to find the snow in good condition for dog sledding, and they had cached 300 lbs. weight of mountain provisions at 11,000 feet. They could therefore afford to wait till the days lengthened before venturing on a final climb. Here is Mr. Belmore Browne's picture of the landscape :—

" The mountain country at the northern base of Mount McKinley is the most beautiful stretch of wilderness that I have ever seen, and I will never forget those wonderful days when I followed up the velvety valleys or clambered among the high rocky peaks as my fancy led me. In the late evening I have trotted downward through valleys that were so beautiful that I was forced against my will to lie down in the soft grass and drink in the wild beauty of the spot, although I knew that I would be late for supper, and that the stove would be cold. The mountains were bare of vegetation, with the exception of velvety carpets of green grass that swept downward from the snow-fields ; in the centres of the cup-shaped hollows ran

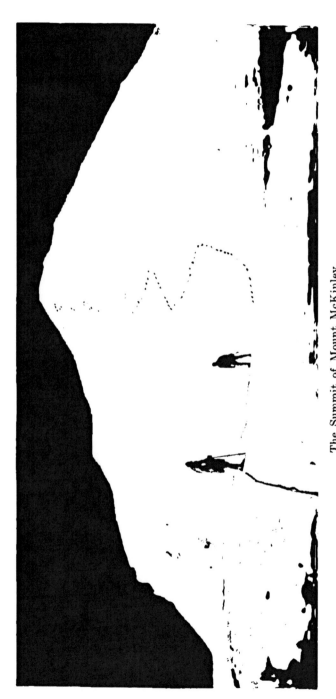

The Summit of Mount McKinley.

(From photographs by Mr. Belmore Browne. By permission of Messrs. Putnam's Sons.)

streams of crystal-clear water ; as the sun sank lower and lower the hills would turn a darker blue, until the cold, clean air from the snow-fields would remind you that night was come and that camp was far away."

The sight of big avalanches on Mount McKinley warned the explorers that great risks had to be faced. On the 5th day of June they started out for their final attack. Unfortunately the weather became very bad, and soon they were enveloped in a heavy snow-storm. Mr. La Voy had hurt his knee hunting, and the ascent through the *seracs* was for him very arduous. The nervous strain, too, was great, for they had to be perpetually on the outlook for avalanches. They feared that one might have buried their cache, and it was an immense relief when they reached the 11,000-feet point and saw the top of their sled sticking out of the snow.

They now moved their supplies up to a camp on the col of the ridge at a height of 11,800 feet. On 19th June they made a reconnaissance, taking with them food for six days, and intending to climb up to the big basin between the two main peaks. They reached a height of 13,200 feet up a sensational *arête*, when Mr. La Voy's knee gave out and they were compelled to return. Three days later they made a camp on the ridge at 13,600 feet. It was a wild and most laborious journey, with a drop of 5,000 feet on the left and of 2,000 on the right. It would take them two hours of hard work to make 500 feet. Apart from the handicap of Mr. La Voy's knee, Mr. Belmore Browne's eyes were very bad. They now realized that they could not reach the summit with their food supply of six days' rations, and they were forced to change their plans, and go back for more food.

They returned to the camp on the col and packed up ten days' rations. With tremendous difficulty they transported them up to a 15,000-feet camp on the ridge, where they were on the edge of the big glacier-filled basin between the two summits. All three found their health beginning to suffer. The pemmican proved to be impossible food, giving them all violent stomach pains, and they were forced to confine themselves to tea and hard-tack. The cold was intense, and inside the tent, with the alcohol stove burning and the warmth of three bodies, the temperature at 7.30 p.m. was five degrees below zero, and three hours later nineteen degrees below zero. "Despite elaborate precautions," says Mr. Belmore Browne, "I can say in all honesty that I did not have a single night's normal sleep above 15,000 feet on account of the cold." By this time their appearance was, as Mr. La Voy said, " sufficient to frighten children into the straight and narrow path." All were more or less snow-blind, burnt black, unshaven, with lips, noses, and hands swollen, cracked, and bleeding.

On 27th June the packs were carried in relays to just under the last *serac*, which was the highest point in the big basin. The altitude was 16,615 feet. Their one comfort was that a snow-field seemed to lead easily up to the sky-line of the central North-East ridge, and that from there they saw what appeared to be a reasonable gradient to the final summit. On 28th June they rested and prepared for their last effort. They were now convinced that nothing could stop them except storm. The night was fine, and the weather promised well for the morrow. The summit appeared to them to be nearly flat with a slight hummocky rise, which must be the highest point in North America.

On 29th June they left camp at 6 a.m., moving very quietly and steadily and conserving their strength. Mr. La Voy and Mr. Belmore Browne led alternately. Slowly they made their way up the snow slopes at the rate of about 400 feet an hour. At 18,500 feet they stopped and congratulated each other, for they had beaten the Duke of the Abruzzi's record on Mount

St. Elias. Presently they were on the sky-line of the ridge, and looking down on the arena where they had struggled two years before. Now, for the first time, came a threat from the weather. The sky was clear to the north, but from the south a great sea of clouds rolled against the mountain like surf on a shore.

As they moved up the ridge breathing became more difficult. At 19,000 feet they had passed the last rock, and were looking at the summit. It rose as innocently as a snow-covered tennis court, but now the wind was rising and the southern sky darkening, and just at the base of the last lift the gale broke. In a fierce scurry of snow they crawled up the round dome, Mr. La Voy leading and hacking steps. Then came Mr. Belmore Browne's turn, and he realized that his hands were freezing, and that the bitter wind was cutting through his flesh. He dare not get dry mittens from his rucksack lest his hands should be frozen during the change. When his second turn was three-fourths finished, Professor Parker's barometer registered 20,000 feet, and they were within 300 feet of the top.

The rest was an evil dream. To each man the other two seemed to be lost in the ice mist, and the cold was freezing their marrow. The storm was growing fiercer, and as they topped a little rise its full fury burst upon them. The story must be given in Mr. Belmore Browne's own words :—

" The breath was driven from my body, and I held to my axe with stooped shoulders to stand against the gale ; I could not go ahead. As I brushed the frost from my glasses and squinted upward through the stinging snow I saw a sight that will haunt me to my dying day. *The slope above me was no longer steep !* That was all I could see. What it meant I will never know for certain—all I can say is that we were close to the top ! "

There was no going on in the teeth of that gale. The three chopped a seat in the ice, trying to find a shelter ; but they were not huddled there a second before they discovered they were freezing. There was nothing for it but to return, for the snow was obliterating their back trail. Dead tired and sick at heart they began the journey back, and found that the steps they had cut had disappeared. It took them nearly two hours to go down an easy slope of 1,000 feet. They reached the base of the dome, guiding themselves only by the direction of the wind, and at last at 7.35 p.m. crawled into their upper camp. All their apparel down to their underclothes was filled with ice. They were beaten by the wind, and by the wind only. On a conservative estimate its pace was fifty-five miles an hour, and the temperature fifteen degrees below zero. Otherwise they suffered little from the altitude. Mr. Belmore Browne was able to roll and smoke a cigarette between 18,000 and 19,000 feet.

They spent a day in their tent, trying to thaw their clothes. Pemmican they could not touch, their chocolate was finished, and their food was tea, sugar, hardtack, and raisins. It was a cruel fate that they had lost ten days' rations in useless pemmican since leaving their 13,200-feet camp, and they had not only lost the food but carried useless weight.

They made one more attempt on the summit, and reached the base of the final dome; but there another storm assailed them, and, after waiting an hour, they went back. There was now a real risk of being caught with insufficient food in a blizzard which would destroy life, and they made haste down the mountain. They had spent seven days above 15,000 feet, six days above 16,000 feet, and four days above 16,650 feet.

As they descended their health improved, and at last they came off the glacier on to the moraine, and lay down on the bare earth. It was the first time for thirty days that they had lain on anything but snow and ice. They slept like logs till the afternoon, and when they awoke a warm wind was blowing up the pass, carrying with it the smell of grass and flowers. "Never can I forget," says Mr. Belmore Browne, "the flood of emotions that swept over me. Professor Parker and La Voy were equally affected by this first smell of the lowlands, and we were wet-eyed and chattered like children as we prepared our packs for the last stage of our journey."

How dangerous was the climatic condition of the mountain may be judged from what happened on the evening of 6th July. From their camp in the foothills they saw the sky suddenly turn a sickly green. There came a deep rumbling from the Alaskan range, and as they looked the mountains melted into mist and the earth began to heave and roll. In front of them a boulder weighing 200 lbs. broke loose from the earth and moved. The surface of the hills seemed to open and the cracks to spout liquid mud. The whole range was wrapped in dust, and as it cleared they saw the peaks spouting avalanches. Had this earthquake overtaken them on the high ground all must have perished.

III

The story has always seemed to me one of the boldest and most patient adventures in the history of mountaineering. Slowly the travellers fought their way to the discovery of the only practical route. Mount McKinley was conquered, though they had failed to cover the hundred or so feet which would have given them the actual summit. They had blazed the path to the top and solved its mysteries. Only that maleficent blizzard at the last moment robbed them of the full fruit of six years' pioneering.

Next year the actual summit was reached. The late Dr. Hudson Stuck, the Archdeacon of the Yukon, ever since he came to the country nine years before, had contemplated an attempt on the mountain. In the autumn of 1912 he sent on supplies by way of the Kantishna River to a point fifty miles from the base. In March, 1913, he and Mr. W. P. Karstens set out to reach the peak from the north. At their base camp, 4,000 feet up, they made a fresh supply of caribou pemmican which proved more satisfactory than that used by Professor Parker and Mr. Belmore Browne. The road taken was the same as that of their predecessors—up the Muldrow Glacier and then up the central North-East ridge. They found that the earthquake of 1912 had completely changed the character of that ridge, and instead of being a reasonable snow gradient, it had become a confused mass of rock and ice, most difficult to surmount. Bit by bit they forced their way up it till they reached the upper basin, and then, being favoured with clear, bright, still weather, they managed to attain the highest point, the southern summit. There had been a story of two miners, called McGonogall and Anderson, who had reached the top in 1910. Dr. Stuck discovered that the top they had reached was the lesser northern peak, for he saw the remains of their flagstaff.

With this ascent the story of the conquest of Mount McKinley is complete.*

* Dr. Stuck argued with much reason that the present name of the mountain is unsuitable, and that the Indian name " Denali "— which means " the Great One "—should be restored. It is to be feared that the suggestion comes too late in the day. Ever since the expedition of 1906 Mount McKinley has become too familiar a name in the Western Hemisphere to be readily changed for another. The story of the Parker-Browne expedition is contained in *The Conquest of Mount McKinley* (New York, Putnams, 1913), and that of Dr. Stuck in *The Ascent of Denali* (New York, Scribners, 1914).

VII

THE HOLY CITIES OF ISLAM

THE HOLY CITIES OF ISLAM

(*Map*, p. 216.)

THE "spell of far Arabia" has been a potent thing from the days when the Egyptians drew wealth from the spice-land of Punt, and Greek traders brought stories of the gums and jewels of Araby the Blessed. But ever since it became the Holy Land of Islam a veil of secrecy, other than that of its stern climate and inhospitable deserts, has descended upon it. It is one of the oldest of arenas of adventure, and it is still one of the least exploited; indeed, in its great Southern Desert it holds one of the few unriddled mysteries of the globe. Except for the semi-mythical Gregorio, who may be read of in Albuquerque's *Commentaries*, no one who did not profess the creed of Islam has entered its two Holy Cities and lived. But the greatest tale of Arabian exploration is not concerned with Mecca and Medina. It is to be found rather in the journeys of the English soldier Captain Sadlier in Nejd; of Sir Richard Burton in the land of

Midian; of Wallin, who crossed the great Nafud sands; of William Gifford Palgrave, who may, or may not, have been an agent of Napoleon III.; and, above all, of Charles Montague Doughty, who, as an avowed Christian, explored the Northern Hedjaz, and in his *Arabia Deserta* has written one of the foremost classics of travel in the English tongue.

Compared with some of these wanderings, a visit to the Holy Cities was a simple matter, requiring only a firm nerve, a good knowledge of Arabic and of Mohammedan ritual, and a real or professed adherence to the creed of Islam. At the beginning of this century the list of Europeans who had entered Mecca and Medina was a long one. They were mostly renegades— French, English, Irish, Scottish, and Italian. In 1807 a certain Domingo Badia y Leblich of Cadiz, travelling as a Moslem prince called Ali Bey, and probably in the pay of Napoleon, entered Mecca in state; but he had become a genuine Mussulman. In 1815 one Thomas Keith, a deserter from the 72nd Highlanders, was Governor of Medina—surely one of the strangest posts ever held even by a Scot! The great European travellers like Burckhardt, Wallin, and Burton went to the Holy Cities in order that by attaining the rank and fame of a Hadji they might win an advantage for

travelling in other Moslem lands. More than one of
them has described minutely the interior of both Mecca
and Medina and the ritual of the great ceremonies.
The Holy Places, though few Western eyes had seen
them, were sufficiently well known to the Western
world. Their true unveiling may be said to have come
about during the Great War, when Hussein, the Sherif
of Mecca, fought as an ally with the British, and, as
King of the Hedjaz, proclaimed his independence of
Turkey.

Yet one journey was taken just before the Great War
which must rank by itself. It told the world nothing
that was not known before ; but it had the merit of
giving a picture of Mecca and Medina under the latest
conditions—a picture drawn with such vigour and in
such detail that it may fairly claim to have revealed
the Holy Cities in a new light to the ordinary man.

Mr. A. J. B. Wavell greatly distinguished himself
in command of Arab scouts in East Africa in the early
part of the Great War, and was responsible for the
brilliant affair at Gazi. In that campaign he gave
his life for his country.* He had been at Winchester,
and in 1908, when he made the plan for visiting Mecca,

* He fell on January 8, 1916.

had been living for some time at Mombasa, where he had acquired Arabic and Swahili, and a considerable knowledge of Moslem customs. His motive was partly curiosity, partly, as he says, to accustom himself to Arab ways, with a view to further explorations in Arabia, and partly in order to obtain the useful prestige of a Hadji. He chose as his companions a certain Abdul Wahid, an Arab from Aleppo who was established in Berlin, and Masaudi, a Mombasa native. The three met at Marseilles on September 23, 1908. They started in good time, for though the pilgrimage was not to take place till the beginning of the following January, Mr. Wavell wanted to go first to Medina, and also to prepare himself by a preliminary discipline in Eastern life. He managed to secure a Turkish passport, which described him as one Ali bin Mohammed, aged twenty-five, a subject of Zanzibar on his way to Mecca.

The three found a vessel at Genoa which took them to Alexandria, where they managed, not without trouble, to get their medicine chest, pistols, and ammunition past the Customs. They then took passages on a Khedivial mail ship for Beyrout. Mr. Wavell had feared that the language difficulty would be serious, but he found it less formidable than he

expected, since the dialects of Arabic are many. He
explained to those who found imperfections in his
accent that in Zanzibar the colloquial language was
Swahili and that no one talked Arabic ; and on the few
occasions when he had to speak Swahili he inverted the
story, announcing that, having been born in Muscat,
his real language was Arabic. As Sir Richard Burton
discovered in his own journey, it was rare indeed to
find any one sufficiently well acquainted with both
languages to find him out. Meantime he had changed
at Alexandria into Arab clothes and shaved his head.

They reached Beyrout safely, and proceeded at once
by rail to Damascus. As they did not propose to
start for Medina for some weeks, they took rooms and
settled down, devoting great attention to the various
Moslem ceremonies, and picking up the right kind of
phrases and quotations and greetings. It is on such
small things that the efficacy of a disguise depends.
"There are nearly as many white men at Mecca,"
Mr. Wavell writes in his account of his adventures,*
"as there are men black or brown in colour. Syrian
' Arabs ' not infrequently have fair hair and blue eyes,
as likewise have some of the natives of the Holy Cities
themselves. I was once asked what colour I stained

* *A Modern Pilgrim in Mecca*, by A. J. B. Wavell (Constable, 1912).

myself for this journey. The question reveals the curious ignorance that lies at the bottom of the so-called race prejudice, of which some people are so proud. You might as well black yourself all over to play Hamlet ! "

Abdul Wahid had brought letters of introduction to a local merchant, who was most hospitable, and supervised the preparations for the journey. They passed safely through the period of Ramadan, and so complete was Mr. Wavell's get-up, and so stalwart his Moslem respectability, that it was with some difficulty that he prevented a middle-aged lady and her two daughters from joining his party for the pilgrimage. He bought the "Ihram," the white robes which are required when entering Mecca, a full camp equipment, and a certain number of stores, and deposited his money with his merchant friend, who gave him two cheques on his agents, one at Medina and one at Mecca. He proposed to travel to Medina by the Hedjaz railway, a very different method from those used by earlier adventurers when aiming at Mecca.

The third-class carriages were desperately crowded, and the train started to the accompaniment of gramo-phones—a modern invention which is very popular in the Hedjaz. On the way Mr. Wavell had a touch of malaria, and his fellow pilgrims showed him every kindness. Presently the train reached Medain Salih, the boundary of the Hedjaz, which no infidel is permitted to pass. On the fourth day the rocky hills opened, and through a gap appeared the minarets of the Prophet's mosque. They arrived at Medina in the middle of a battle, for the Turkish garrison had come to loggerheads with the neighbouring Bedawin, and the Holy City was more or less in a state of siege. The railway was spoiling trade for the neighbouring tribes, and they were demanding compensation, which Constantinople would not pay.

Medina lies in an open plain some 3,000 feet above sea-level. To the south the country is open, but on the north and west, between five and ten miles distant, rise rocky mountains. The city, which has a population of some 30,000, lives entirely on the pilgrims, as an English watering-place lives on summer visitors. The pilgrims are classified by their lands of origin, and there are official guides, called Mutowifs, attached to each group. The first trouble arose from these guides. If Mr. Wavell went about with the Zanzibar Mutowifs he was certain to meet some one who knew him in Mombasa, even if he were not caught out in the language. So it was arranged that Abdul Wahid should profess to come from Bagdad, while Mr. Wavell passed as "a Derweish," and Masaudi as his slave. A "Derweish," which denotes properly a member of certain monastic orders, is a title occasionally assumed by pilgrims who do not wish to be identified with any particular nationality.

Happily, at the station there were no Zanzibar guides, and the party were able to find rooms in a retired corner at the moderate rate of £2 a month. The landlord was an Abyssinian called Iman, a man of some private means, who had been captured as a child by Arab slavers and sold in Mecca. He proved a most useful friend to the party during their stay.

So began a curious life of endless religious observations. Apart from the sacred places, which few European eyes had beheld, there was a perpetual interest in the study of the pilgrims. "A large caravan came in from Yembu, bringing crowds of Indians, Javanese, and Chinamen. Every Eastern race might be identified in the motley crowd, and every variety of costume, till the whole resembled nothing so much as a fancy dress ball. In the same line of prayer stand European Turks, with their frock coats and stick-up collars; Anatolians, with enormous trousers and fantastic weapons; Arabs from the West, who look as if they were arrayed for burial; the Bedou (Bedawin), with their spears and scimitars; and Indians, who, in spite of their being the richest class there, managed, as usual, to look the most unkempt and the least clean. Then, besides, were the Persians, Chinese, Javanese, Japanese, Malayans, a dozen different African races, Egyptians, Afghans, Baluchies, Swahilis, and ' Arabs ' of every description." Representatives of half the races of the globe may be picked out in the mosque any day during the month before the pilgrimage.

The behaviour of the pilgrims, who now saw with their own eyes the tomb of the Prophet, which from their childhood they had been taught to regard with awe, was a proof of the living reality of the Islamic faith. " Many burst into tears and frantically kissed the railings : I have seen Indians and Afghans fall down apparently unconscious. They seem to be much more affected here than before the Kaaba itself. At Mecca the feeling is of awe and reverence; here the personal element comes in. The onlooker might fancy that they were visiting the tomb of some dear friend, one whom they had actually known and been intimate with in his lifetime. With frantic interest they listen to their guides as they describe the surroundings.

Here is the place where the Prophet prayed, the pulpit he preached from, the pillar against which he leant; there, looking to the mosque, is the window of Abu Bakar's house, where for long he stayed as a guest; and beyond is the little garden planted by his daughter Fatima." Moreover, there is no suggestion of infidel authority, the Moslem standards float over the town, Moslem cannon protect its gates, and no unbeliever may enter. But there are startling touches of modernity. In the shops you may buy European tinned goods and note advertisements of Cadbury's chocolates and Huntley and Palmer's biscuits!

The party had brought introductions from Damascus and Abdul Wahid had made various friends, so they saw a good deal of society. The time was just after the rising of the Young Turks and the grant of the Constitution. Mr. Wavell, who was a staunch Tory, found to his disgust that every one talked parliamentarianism and Liberal principles. England and the English were everywhere in high favour because of our attitude in the recent quarrel with Austria over the annexation of Bosnia. "I am afraid I managed to give the impression that Zanzibar is a sadly backward state, or that I myself am peculiarly stupid. Not to know a word of any European language is to

be held very ignorant, even in Medina. Most people
of the class with whom I associated had at any rate
a smattering of French, and sometimes of English too.
I was careful never to know anything."

Their stay in Medina was much enlivened by the
Bedawin siege. Mr. Wavell tried to get enlisted in
the defence force, and when that plan failed, succeeded in getting into a very warm corner just outside
the gates. They visited like industrious tourists every
possible place of interest, and few pilgrims can have
spent a more enlightening three weeks. During the
whole time they were never in real danger. They
had, indeed, a scuffle with a Persian Mutowif, who
would insist that Mr. Wavell was a Persian; but
by vigorous bluffing they made him apologize, and
afterwards employed him as a guide. Once only
was there a hint of trouble. Masaudi, standing in
the mosque one day before the noonday prayer, found
himself face to face with five Mombasa Swahilis who
knew him intimately, and, what was worse, knew
Mr. Wavell. Masaudi showed remarkable gifts of
mendacity. He said he had left Mr. Wavell in England, and having saved a little money thought the
present was a good time to perform the pilgrimage.
He was in Medina, he said, as a servant of some rich

Egyptian pilgrims. As he walked back after prayer he dropped his string of beads. The Swahilis asked where his house was, and he promised to show it them; but half-way up the street he suddenly remembered the beads, bolted back, and lost himself in the crowd.

The incident convinced Mr. Wavell that he had better start without delay for Mecca. Their plan was to go to the coast at Yembu, for which a caravan was starting at once. They arranged for three camels, one to carry a *shugduf*, which is a cross between a pannier and a howdah, and the other two for luggage; and they bought the necessary food. They took with them a Persian called Jaffa as cook, and his brother Ibrahim as general servant. The luggage was carried down to the big square where the caravan was parked, and where the travellers had to pass the night. That evening there occurred an untoward event. Mr. Wavell was going to a shop for some small purchase, when he met two Mutowifs who demanded to know his nationality. The Mutowifs, being a strict trades union, were convinced that he was defrauding the brotherhood. He took a high line and showed his pistol, and, fortunately, his late landlord came down the street at the moment

View of Medina.

(By permission of Messrs. Arch. Constable & Co., Ltd.)

and took his side. What might have been an ugly experience ended in a minor street brawl.

The journey to Yembu was little better than a nightmare. The fashionable road from Medina to Mecca is overland, or back to Damascus and so direct to Jiddah by the Suez Canal. Only poor people go by the Yembu route, which is supposed to be the most hazardous and the roughest in the Hedjaz. There were no escort or police arrangements, no daily market, and each traveller had to carry his own provisions and water. The Bedawin hired out the camels, which numbered about 5,000, and a Bedawi sheikh was in charge. The countryside was infested by robbers who constantly cut off stragglers. The ground, too, was difficult going, being a rough mountain-land, and, while the noons were scorching, the nights were bitterly cold. Every night an encampment was made, roughly circular in shape, into which the whole caravan was packed in the smallest possible space. " While I was trying to get warm a man stumbled against me and nearly knocked me into the fire. Turning round, I was shocked to see a figure, stained almost from head to foot with blood from a tremendous gash in the head, obviously a sword cut. He asked for water, and I went into the tent to get him some, but returning, found him gone. We heard the next day that no less than six men had been murdered that night and many others wounded ; and so it went on till we reached Yembu. These unfortunates were mostly people who could not afford camels, and so had to perform the journey on foot. Straying from the main body in search of firewood they got picked up by the marauders hanging on the flanks, who seized every opportunity to plunder such stragglers of their miserable possessions, and killed unhesitatingly any who resisted."

It was in this country that Charles Doughty spent part of his time, and Mr. Wavell thinks that one reason of his success was that he carried nothing worth stealing. The fact that Doughty denied neither his religion nor his nationality seemed to him not the most remarkable fact about the achievement. "The Bedou themselves are not fanatical on these points, and he did not attempt to enter the forbidden cities. Of course, the fact of a stranger being a Christian is always a good excuse for knocking him on the head ; but failing it they will soon find another if they want to do so, and will be quite uninfluenced by it if they don't."

They had one row with their camel man, Saad, who

tried to extort bakhsheesh. Suddenly he quieted down, and became all politeness to the end of the journey. The reason for this was that that resourceful liar Ibrahim had told him that Mr. Wavell was a nephew of the Governor of Yembu. This story served the travellers well. It spread through the caravan, and many of the pilgrims who were being blackmailed by their camel-men came to him and begged his protection, and received it. At last, on the dawn of the sixth day, after trekking without a stop for the last twenty hours, they reached the gates of Yembu.

Here they were delayed some time, owing to the fact that the pilgrim ship to take them to Jiddah—an old Greek vessel chartered by a syndicate of Persians—would not start till its owners considered that sufficient pilgrims had arrived. Abdul Wahid now became the popular leader. At the head of a mob of passengers he seized the Persians and carried them off to the Governor. Mounted on a pile of sugar bags he delivered an impassioned address, concluding with " We had better be dealing with Christians than Moslems, who cheat their brethren in this fashion." " Murmurs of protest," says Mr. Wavell, " deprecated this revolting comparison. We all thought he was going a little too far." The Persians finally capitulated, and the ship got under way. But there came one last *contretemps*. A party of Megribi Arabs had passed the quarantine and were half-way out to the ship when one of them died. The shore authorities refused to let them land again and the Persians declined to take the corpse aboard. The Arabs could not throw it into the sea because there were certain ceremonial washings to be performed and certain prayers to be said. An Egyptian lawyer on board gave it as his opinion that the man, having taken his ticket, was entitled to his passage, dead or alive, there being no saving clause in the contract. Finally the Megribis got sick of arguing, swarmed over the bulwarks, and hoisted up their departed comrade. Their fierce faces and long knives settled the point of law.

At half-past four in the afternoon the syren blew to announce that the pilgrims were within that latitude where they must exchange their ordinary clothes for the Ihram—the garb which has to be worn by all travellers who attain a certain distance from Mecca. The costume consists of two white bath towels, one worn round the loins and the other over the shoulders. The head is unprotected, but deaths from sunstroke are singularly few. The costume is not becoming, especially in the case of a fat man. " A party of

elderly European Turks, close to us looked peculiarly
ludicrous, their appearance suggesting members of
the Athenæum Club suddenly evicted from a Turkish
bath."

The party remained four days at Jiddah, visiting
among other places the tomb of Eve, who apparently
was about a quarter of a mile in height, so it was a
tiring business to make the necessary perambulation of
her sepulchre. Owing to their behaviour at Yembu
they had acquired much *kudos* among the pilgrims and
had no difficulties during their stay. The only anxiety
was about the Mombasa Swahilis, and also about a
certain Mombasa sheikh who knew Mr. Wavell and
was proposing to go to Mecca that year. As neither
sheikh nor Swahilis arrived, they decided to risk it
and go on to Mecca, after Mr. Wavell had left a letter
for the sheikh requesting him to hold his tongue.
They found a Mutowif who was a local agent of one
of the principal Mecca guides, to whom he wrote
recommending them. They never intended to employ
this guide, but the recommendation gave them an
excuse to refuse to employ others. Having taken
every precaution they could think of, they prepared
for the last stage of the journey. "Abdul Wahid
made a vow that if he returned safely he would present

three dollars to the poor of Jiddah. We told him we thought he was asking the Almighty to do it too cheaply and that he had much better make it a sovereign. To our disgust, when he did get back, he utterly declined to disgorge the promised sum.

The journey from Jiddah to Mecca can be performed in a day, for it is only some forty miles. The road is protected by a line of blockhouses, every mile or so there is a restaurant or a booth for refreshment, and all day long during the pilgrimage season there is a continuous caravan. A strange silence broods over everything. There is no shouting or singing or firing of guns, and the camels move over the deep soft sand with scarcely a sound, for to the Moslem it is the approach to the holy of holies. "To him it is a place hardly belonging to this world, overshadowed like the Tabernacle of old by the almost tangible presence of the deity. Five times daily throughout his life has he turned his face towards this city, whose mysteries he is now about to view with his own eyes. Moreover, according to the common belief, pilgrimage brings certain responsibilities and even perils along with its manifold blessings. Good deeds in Mecca count many thousand times their value elsewhere, but sin that is committed there will reap its reward in hell." Mr. Wavell and his companions, decently but simply clad in their bath towels, approached the city repeating the ceremonial prayers. To one which began, " O Lord, Who hast brought me in safety to this place, do Thou bring me safely out again," he said a fervid " Amen."

Mecca lies in a deep-cut hollow of the hills, and is not visible till travellers are at its gates. Presently they found themselves in the great square which contains the Kaaba, the black covering of which is in startling contrast with the dazzling white marble of the pavement. The Kaaba itself is a cube about forty feet square, built of granite blocks, and let into the wall is a great black stone. This stone is believed to have fallen from heaven, which it probably did, as it is clearly a meteorite. Barefooted, the little party moved round it the requisite seven times, chanting the proper prayers. Then a small circular patch of hair was shaved from their heads, and the first part of the ceremony was over.

Mecca was then under the semi-independent rule of Sherif Hussein, and, on the whole, seemed to be well governed ; but the problem of the municipal authorities in looking after the vast crowd of pilgrims was no easy one. As at Medina, every race on earth was represented there. Mr. Wavell was most struck by the Javanese, who were present in great numbers, for there was then a strong Islamic revival in the Far East. The party found comfortable lodgings in a quiet street, and, as at Medina, went much into society, owing to the wide acquaintance of Abdul Wahid. Mecca is one of the few places remaining where there is an open slave-market, and female slaves may be bought for prices ranging from £20 to £100, though Georgians and Circassians fetch more. Masaudi discovered an acquaintance in a boy called Kepi from Mombasa, whose father had died on the pilgrimage, and was now left destitute. Kepi was accordingly attached to the party. Mr. Wavell heard the good news that the Mombasa sheikh, whose coming he had been warned of, had now written saying that he would not arrive that year.

The time passed pleasantly in sight-seeing and giving and receiving hospitality. Mr. Wavell gave one dinner to no less than twelve guests, which, since he had an excellent cook, was very successful. There are few more curious incidents in the literature of travel than this party given by a disguised Christian in the Moslem holy of holies to a company which

View of Mecca.

(By permission of Messrs. Arch. Constable & Co., Ltd.)

included Arabs from Bussorah and Mecca, two Persian
merchants, and a Turkish officer from the Bagdad
Corps. Most Western luxuries can be obtained in
Mecca, including ice cream, which, according to Mr.
Wavell, is a frozen mixture of tinned milk, dirty water,
and cholera germs ! Alcoholic liquor can also be got
if you know where to go for it.

The great festival was now approaching. A white
linen band was fastened round the black covering of
the Kaaba, which remained there till the great day,
when the covering was changed. A new covering is
brought every year from Egypt, made of dull black
silk and cotton, embroidered with the name of God
on every square foot. It is prepared in Constantinople, and is said to cost £3,600. The main ceremony
of the festival is as follows : On a certain fixed day
all adults must leave the city before nightfall, and go
to a village called Mina, some five miles to the north.
They pass the night there, and go nine miles farther
on the next morning to Mount Arafat, where they
remain till sunset. They then return, and sleep at
Nimrah, half-way between Arafat and Mina. The
third day they must be back at Mina in the morning,
go through the ceremony of throwing stones at the
Three Devils, proceed to Mecca for other ceremonies,

and return to Mina for the night. The fourth day is spent at Mina, and at noon on the fifth day they return to Mecca. The bath towels of the Ihram are now relinquished, and the pilgrim dons the best new clothes which he can afford. He is then entitled to the name of Hadji, and thereafter through life can wear a special headgear, such as a green turban.

The exodus from the city to Mina was a strange sight. The different holy carpets were escorted by regiments and brass bands, that of Egypt marching to the tune of the " Barren Rocks of Aden." Sherif Hussein was there on horseback, accompanied by a crowd of spearmen and a squadron of racing camels. The ride to Mina beggared description. "The best idea of what it is like," Mr. Wavell wrote, " will be gained by considering that at least half a million people are traversing these nine miles of road between sunrise and ten o'clock this day ; that about half of them are mounted, and that many of them possess baggage animals as well. The roar of this great column is like a breaking sea, and the dust spreads for miles over the surrounding country. When, passing through the second defile, we came in sight of Arafat itself, the spectacle was stranger still. The hill was literally black with people, and tents were springing up around it, hundreds to the minute, in an ever-widening circle. As we approached, the dull murmur caused by thousands of people shouting the formula, ' Lebéka, lebéka, Allahooma lebéka,' which had long been audible, became so loud that it dominated every other sound. In the distance it sounded rather ominous, suggestive of some deep disturbance of great power, like the rumble of an earthquake."

The hygienic conditions of the exodus were of course abominable. Tanks and springs were soon fouled by people bathing in them, and the condition of the hill-side was filthy beyond description. Often some infectious disease like cholera decimates the pilgrims, but our travellers were fortunate in escaping it. They went through all the proper ceremonies, and stoned the Three Devils at Mina with gusto. The Three Devils are three stone pillars, and, in a mob of many thousands of bad shots, a good many pilgrims are bound to suffer. They bought a sheep to sacrifice, like the others, and a mess of offal and blood was soon added to the attractions of the countryside. They then went back to Mecca, kissed the Black Stone, had another square inch of hair shaved from their temples, and were free to put off the bath towels. Now was the moment for the new clothes. Abdul Wahid appeared in a bilious yellow garment brought from Damascus ; Masaudi in an obsolete regimental mess waistcoat ; while Mr. Wavell was chastely arrayed in white cloth robes, a black jubba, and a gold sash with a dagger.

Thus attired they set out again for Mina for the last ceremonies. In the night a thief got into their tent, and carried off Masaudi's new turban, £5 in gold, and various oddments, including a couple of pistols. In the morning they went to salute the Sherif, and when they had returned and were sitting in their tent, passed through the most dangerous moment of the adventure. The wall of the tent was down, as is usual in the heat of the day, and they were squatting on the carpet, when suddenly they heard an exclamation from Masaudi. Looking round, they saw, standing within a few feet of them and looking straight into the tent, three of the Mombasa Swahilis whom they had met at Medina. It scarcely seemed possible that they could miss seeing Masaudi, and if they did they would certainly come into the tent to greet him, when Mr. Wavell was bound to be recognized. The morning sun, however, was shining right in their eyes, so they saw nothing, and passed on. As soon as they had turned their backs Mr. Wavell and Masaudi ran out of the tent on the other side and mingled with the crowd. They returned to Mecca, to be congratulated by their friends on the successfully accomplished pilgrimage, and Mr. Wavell was free to go into the world as Hadji Ali bin Mohammed.

It was now their business to get out of Mecca as soon as possible, especially as money was running low. They paid the necessary farewell visits, hired the transport, and started, intending to do the journey in one day. They were, however, held up by a sentry on the road, and had to spend a cold and comfortless night in the open, and did not enter Jiddah till sunrise. At Jiddah they separated ; Masaudi went to Mombasa, Abdul Wahid to Persia, and Mr. Wavell to Egypt.

In summing up the expedition, Mr. Wavell was disposed to attribute his success not to any histrionic gifts of his own, but to the ignorance of the inhabitants of the Holy Cities, and their lack of interest in the outside world, even the Islamic world. " There are so many different sects in Islam, and its adherents are found in so many different countries, that I seriously believe that if some one invented for himself a country and a language that did not exist at all, and journeyed thus to Mecca, no one there would know enough geography to find him out. Yet with all, they are quick enough in their way, and if some Mutowif would take the trouble to write a book on ethnography in its relation to the Islam of to-day, and classify the different races that come to Mecca, such a deception as I practised would become impossible." They did, as a matter of fact, excite a certain suspicion, and their two servants, though they were Persians and knew little Arabic, must have had their own views. The great assets of the travellers were their knowledge of Arabic and Moslem ceremonial, and the fact that Mr. Wavell took up his disguise long before he approached the Hedjaz. He considered that Medina was much the more dangerous place of the two, and that no traveller should go there who was not thoroughly at home in his oriental character.

Whatever may be said, the journey is one of extreme danger and delicacy, and demands not only great knowledge, but perpetual vigilance. It must be remembered that a European is all the time in the midst of a fanatical and devout people, and that the highest merit would be acquired by any one who might discover and denounce the unbeliever. In spite of every precaution there must be an enormous element of luck, and Mr. Wavell's conclusion is that his escape was due rather to a series of happy chances than to his own good management.

VIII

THE EXPLORATION OF NEW GUINEA

THE EXPLORATION OF NEW GUINEA

(*Map*, p. 248.)

ALMOST every part of the globe has suffered some change in the past century. It may have altered its appearance by settlement and cultivation and the growth of cities; or, if it still remains a wilderness, there are routes of commerce through it which bring it to the knowledge of the world. But the great island of New Guinea is almost as little changed to-day by the advent of white adventurers as when, in the year 1527, Jorge de Meneses, the Portuguese Governor of the Spice Islands, first landed on its swampy shores. In 1545, eighteen years later, it received the name by which it is known to-day. The Portuguese Empire decayed, and during the seventeenth century the Dutch appeared. In the eighteenth century many famous voyagers, like Dampier, Carteret, and Captain Cook, touched the island, and in the last century the rapid opening up of the world by travellers and missionaries bore fruit even in those remote seas. The Dutch held the western end; in 1884 Germany laid claim to the north-eastern part; and that same year the south-eastern section, which had been formally taken over in 1883 by Queensland, was annexed to the British Crown. In 1899 the Dutch boundary was delimited, and Holland, with the assent of the Powers, assumed direct control of her share. The one change to-day in these arrangements is that the former German section is now administered under mandate by the Commonwealth of Australia.

The first decade of this century saw great exploring activity on the part of all three European masters. The Dutch especially did excellent work, and Dr. Lorentz was the first man to reach the snows of the inland mountains. But few of the secrets of the island—geographical, zoological, and botanical—have yet been unriddled. The place is so remote from Europe, its climate is so deadly, its inhabitants so treacherous, and its forests and swamps so impenetrable, that exploration there is in many ways a more desperate undertaking than anywhere else on the globe.

I have selected two expeditions as an example of what the pioneer must undergo. In 1910 the Ornithologists' Union sent out an expedition to investigate

the New Guinea fauna and collect specimens. Captain
Cecil Rawling, whose thirst for the unknown was un-
quenchable, accompanied it on the geographical side,
and Mr. A. F. R. Wollaston as medical officer. There
was no proper survey equipment, as the mission was
primarily one of naturalists. Ten Gurkhas were enlisted from India, and the Dutch Government supplied a certain number of Javanese troops. Coolies
also were recruited in Java, who turned out to be
hopelessly unsuitable both in physique and character
for any serious travel in the wilds. The majority
were about sixteen years of age, and they appeared
in the jungle decently dressed in black frock coats
and bowler hats !

The part selected was the southern coast of the
Dutch territory, and it was Captain Rawling's hope
that they would be able to penetrate to that belt of
snow mountains, at the head of the coastal rivers,
running from the Nassau Range in the west to
Wilhelmina Peak in the east, where Dr. Lorentz had
been the pioneer. Obviously it was vital to find a
river which would take them direct to the hills. But
they had no previous information to go upon, and
were compelled to select their stream at random.
Had they gone farther east, and chosen the Utakwa,

they would have found a current navigable for an ocean-going steamer for seventeen miles from its mouth, and for launches for many miles more—a river, moreover, running directly from the highest snows of Mount Carstensz. As it was, they hit upon a river called the Mimika, a small jungle-fed stream rising in the low foothills sixty miles to the west of Carstensz, and twenty miles or so short of the main range. The Mimika, too, was full of endless windings and liable to sudden and violent floodings. Hence it was of little use to the expedition in the way of transport. This was the more regrettable since transport was the essence of the problem. From the foothills of the mountains to the sea lies a belt of forest like a barbed-wire entanglement. This forest is so dense that the cutting of a road can only progress at the rate of 100 yards a day. It is swampy, and often, in flood-time, under water, and filled with every form of noxious insect life. Unless this nightmare land can be circumvented by the use of a broad river channel, it must take even a strong party many months before they reach the base of the hills.

This was what happened to Captain Rawling. On January 26, 1910, after a base camp had been established at Wakatimi, not far from the Mimika mouth,

he set off to ascend the river. Here is his description
of the country :—

"It is quite impossible for any one who has not visited
these parts of New Guinea to realize the density of the forest
growth. The vegetation, through which only the scantiest
glimpses of the sky can be obtained, appears to form, as it
were, two great horizontal strata. The first comprises the
giant trees, whose topmost boughs are 150 feet or more above
the ground ; the other, the bushes, shrubs, and trees of lesser
growth, which never attain a greater height than 30 to 40 feet.
Such is the richness of the soil that not one square foot remains untenanted, and the never-ending struggle to reach
upwards towards the longed-for light goes on silently and
relentlessly. Creepers and parasites in endless variety cling
to every stem, slowly but surely throttling their hosts. From
tree to tree their tentacles stretch out, seizing on to the first
projecting branch and limb, and forming such a close and
tangled mass that the dead and dying giants of the forest
are prevented from falling to the ground. . . .

"The various devices recommended in the books of one's
childhood, and, it may be added, in learned books as well,
whereby the traveller is enabled to recover a lost trail or
regain the right direction, are here of no avail. For instance,
moss does not grow more on one side of a tree-trunk than on
the other ; trees do not lean away from the prevailing wind ;
nor is the position of the sun a guide, for it is seldom visible.
In fact, the traveller has nothing to rely upon but the compass
or a local guide, and even the latter is often at fault. Hopeless indeed does the outlook appear when the wanderer,
hedged in by a wall of scrub and creeper which limits his
vision to a distance of ten or twelve yards, realizes that he
has lost his bearings ; when the vastness of the forest seems
to press upon him, and there is no sound to be heard but the

drip, drip of the water-laden trees and the bubbling of the stinking bog underfoot. His only chance of escape is to find a stream, and follow it down till it joins a main river."

The first big episode was the discovery of the Pygmies who lived in the foothills, and were assiduously hunted by the forest tribes. The average height of these little men was 4 feet 7 inches, and Captain Rawling penetrated to their village in a clearing above the head waters of the Mimika. The Mimika source was reached, but led them nowhere, and they fared no better with another small stream to the west, called the Kapare. Then by accident a secret native path was discovered running eastward—a mere tunnel in the matted forest. By this route they were able to reach a parallel river, called the Tuaba, which was a tributary of the larger Kamura. From a village called Ibo as a centre, the expedition made various casts east and north, but found it impossible to get near the skirts of the hills.

Captain Rawling returned to the coast and made excursions along the eastern shore, but found no adjacent river mouth which promised better. By this time it was June, and the floods began with such vigour that practically the whole country between the mountains and the sea was under water. When the floods ebbed, a resolute attempt was made to push east from Ibo, and with a good deal of trouble another parallel stream was reached, called the Wataikwa. The party founded a camp there, and explored the upper waters of that stream. Travelling was extremely difficult, because the only decent road was the river bed, and this route was promptly made impossible by a new spate. The travellers had to face the fact that the farther they went eastward the greater became the labour of carrying supplies, for their base camp remained on the Mimika.

Still, an effort must be made unless the expedition was to admit failure. It was decided that the best plan was to try and cut a road through the forest to the next stream on the east, in the hope that it would lead them into the hills. This was done, and the Iwaka River was reached after much severe toil. They had entered a desperate country, strewn with moss-covered boulders and seamed with gullies covered with an impenetrable mass of timber. The density of this growth was unbelievable ; through it no man could force a way unless with an axe in hand, and as most of the trees were of very hard wood—the stems varying from four to eight inches in diameter—and clothed from top to bottom with damp earth covered with moss, progress at times became impossible. An idea of the labour involved in the task of clearing a two-foot path through this forest may be judged by the fact that a stretch of five thousand yards required three weeks' constant work before a man could pass freely along. On one day two cutters achieved a length of two hundred and ten yards, and on another, when Captain Rawling was working by himself, all he could add was a piece of ninety yards in length. No wonder he asks, " Can this forest, with its horrible monotony and impregnability, be equalled by any other in the world ? "

Down came the rain again, and in August the country was all under water. The advance was not renewed till the beginning of 1911, when fresh supplies had arrived from England, and the old motor-boat had been put in repair. So far, a year's hard labour had not taken the explorers within measurable distance of their goal. With the help of a launch, food supplies for eight weeks were stored at the head of the Mimika. One story may be quoted as a piece of comic relief in a very grim campaign. On 4th January two men quarrelled in camp and killed each other.

" The sergeant who, by the way, was a foreigner, took charge of the burial ceremonials, and was evidently quite

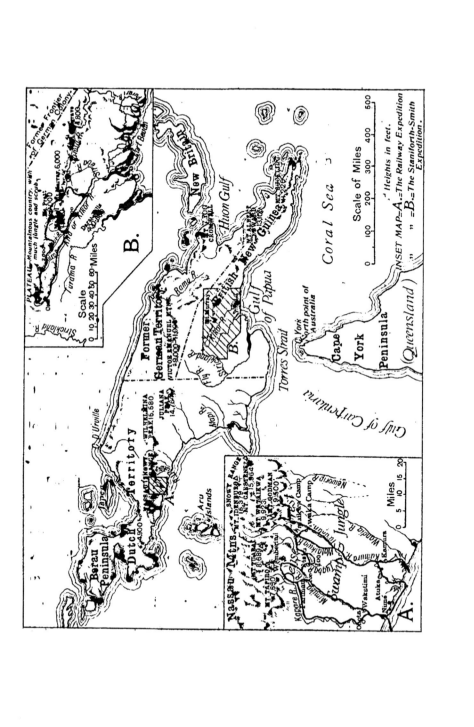

determined that, for his part, nothing should be lacking which the importance of the occasion demanded. Drawing his sword, and placing himself between the graves, he harangued the spectators. ' Men,' he said, ' this day two servants of the Government have lost their lives at the hands of each other. Were they not both good men ? hein.' ' One man very bad man,' chipped in an officious convict, but a glance from the offended sergeant made him wish that he had never spoken. ' Whether they will both go to heaven I cannot say,' exclaimed he, ' but I think Allah '—pointing upwards with his sword— ' will first purge them with a fire. Take this as a lesson.' Then, drawing himself up to his full height as befitted the occasion, he returned his sword with a clank to the scabbard, and, as far as the public was concerned, the ceremony was at an end. The sergeant, however, had not yet finished. Returning to his hut, he refreshed himself with a few glasses of gin, and played on the mouth-organ the national anthems of the three flags under which he had served. This terminated the funeral obsequies, and with the exception of the official report and the entry in the accounts ' To one bottle gin for disinfecting corpse,' nothing remained to mark the sanguinary affair."

The Iwaka was safely reached, and the last stage began. At first the advance was up its right bank, but this only brought the travellers back to the upper glen of the Wataikwa, which they had already found impossible. It was clear that the Iwaka must be crossed and the ridges to the east ascended. Getting over that stream was an ugly business, and it was achieved only by the heroism of one of the Gurkhas, who managed to haul himself hand over hand along a thin rope. Captain Rawling records that it was "one of the best actions carried out in cold blood that I have ever had the good fortune to witness." A rough bridge was constructed, and on the morning of February 8, 1911, thirteen months after their first landing on the coast, the party had at last a road to the upper ridges. It was thick, misty weather, and of the farther mountains they only had occasional glimpses. Camp was pitched at an altitude of 5,400 feet, but not on solid ground, for all the climbing had been done on the top of live or dead timber. The following morning they hacked their way to a clear space on the ridge at a height of 5,600 feet, and there they were at last favoured with the view for which they had longed, and were able to fix the position of the main peaks.

Looking southward they saw the sea, and between it and them the dark green of the forest through which they had struggled for so many months. The gloom was broken at rare intervals by a streak of light, which was a river. Nearly five miles away stood Mount Godman, and beyond it the huge southern face of the range, a gigantic black cliff, eighty miles from east to west, with a clear drop of nearly a mile and three-quarters—by far the greatest precipice in the world. Behind this scarp rose the snow mountains—Mount Leonard Darwin, to the north-west, 13,882 feet; and to the north-east Mount Idenburg, 15,379 feet, and the glittering top of Carstensz, which is almost 16,000 feet. The great peaks seemed, below, a mass of wild, black precipices, cleft with fissures; but, above, a long, easy snow-field, curving gently to the summits. It was such a view as the old Portuguese adventurers might have had when, after struggling for months through the coastal jungles, they suddenly came in sight of Kenya or Kilimanjaro. But for Captain Rawling and his party it would be no more than a Pisgah-sight. Advance was impossible. The fatal choice of the Mimika route meant that they had taken the worst road conceivable to the great snows. The attainment of the peaks must be left to their successors. He who would understand the full difficulties and miseries of that expedition must read Captain Rawling's own narrative.*

Rarely has a more thoroughly comfortless expedition been undertaken. To begin with, the food was

* *The Land of the New Guinea Pygmies*, by Captain C. G. Rawling (Seeley, Service, and Co., 1913).

bad and unsuitable, for they had the surplus stores
from Shackleton's Antarctic expedition, and the joys
of bully-beef, pea-soup, and pickles under an equatorial sky may be imagined. It was impossible to
get good local assistance, for the natives were a pre-
posterous race, treacherous and unreliable when they
were not actively malevolent. They were subject to
sudden panics, when they fled to the jungle, and to
wild outbursts of sorrow, when they would weep
and sob for hours. The imported Javanese were, if
possible, more hopeless. Then there was every kind
of noxious insect—mosquitoes without end, gigantic
leeches dangling from every leaf which made a
speciality of attacking the eyeballs, ticks, stinking
caterpillars, immense blue-bottles which swarmed in
clouds over any food left uncovered, crickets which
ate a man's clothes up in a night, and a plague of
minute bees which settled in myriads on the heated
face of the traveller. Above all, there was the rain.
The whole country was water-logged by the flooding
rivers and the incessant deluge. In the dry season
the average rainfall was about two and a half inches
a day! Mr. Wollaston took the trouble to keep a
meteorological diary, and found that during the first
year rain fell on 330 days, and that on 295 days it

New Guinea Canoes.

was accompanied by thunder and lightning. Of the 400 men of all races employed during the first year, 12 per cent. died in the country from hardships, and 83 per cent. of the total force was invalided from New Guinea. Of the Europeans and natives who landed during that year, only eleven lasted out the whole fifteen months of the expedition. Of these eleven, four were Europeans, four Gurkhas, two Javanese soldiers, and one a convict. When it is remembered that eight months is the maximum period allowed by the Dutch authorities for continued service in New Guinea, the marvel is that these eleven escaped with their lives. It was with no regret that Captain Rawling said farewell to what must be by far the most unpleasant land on earth. " Wild shrieks had greeted us on our first arrival in the country, and wild shrieks echoed down the still reach of the river as the boats crept towards the sea."

Mount Carstensz still awaits its conqueror. Since the Rawling expedition much has been done in the exploration of the central mountains. In 1913 Mount Wilhelmina (15,580 feet), of which Dr. Lorentz had trodden the lower snows, was finally ascended by Captain Herderschee. In 1921 Captain Kremer reached the same summit from the north, and found a means of crossing the range at a height of 13,480 feet. A German expedition under Dr. Moszkowski, which was projected in 1913 to attempt Carstensz from the north, was stopped by the war. Meantime, in September, 1912, Mr. Wollaston, Captain Rawling's companion, had returned to New Guinea and ascended the Utakwa River. Its head waters led him direct to Carstensz, and by establishing a series of depots for food in the foothills, he was able to reach the main *massif* of the mountain. Above 8,000 feet he left the jungles behind ; but the mountain proved very difficult, and the rain, as usual, fell without intermission. At 14,200 feet he reached the snow-line, and on February 1, 1913, from a camp above 12,000 feet, he climbed to 14,866 feet, a thousand feet or so below the summit. There he was stopped by an ice fall, and lack of provisions and the weakness of his party prevented him from finding a way to turn it. The top of the mountain is an ice cap which breaks down very sheer on the south side, and Mr. Wollaston is of opinion that the easiest ascent would be from the north. This closes for the present the history of the exploration of Carstensz.

For the second story we move east into British territory. There the general configuration is the same—swamps near the shore, then a tangled forest, then a range of inland mountains, though these are much less conspicuous than the ranges in Dutch territory, and scarcely rise above 6,000 feet. In 1911 the Hon. Miles Staniforth Smith, who had been Mayor of Kalgoorlie, and a senator representing West Australia in the Commonwealth Parliament, and was at the time Administrator of Papua, set out across the centre of the unexplored part of his province to investigate the sources of the rivers emptying into the Papuan Gulf. As the travelling was of the roughest, and the aim was exploration rather than scientific research, the party was kept very small—three white men, Mr. Staniforth Smith, Mr. Bell, the Chief Inspector of Native Affairs, and Mr. Pratt, a Staff Surveyor, together with eleven native police and seventeen carriers. They started from the head of the navigable waters of the Kikor or Aird River, meaning to push north to the top of Mount Murray, and then traverse to the west along the ridge. Mount Murray, which is some 6,000 feet high, was safely reached, and the explorers found themselves moving along a high limestone plateau, much fissured by streams and diversified by parallel ranges. They hoped ultimately to reach the Strickland River, which is a tributary of the great Fly River, and so complete the rest of their journey by rafts.

Presently they found such a river running in a deep gorge, and from certain rapids which had been noted by earlier explorers, they assumed it to be the Strickland. Now began their adventures. The stream seemed to be a series of wild rapids; but as the Strickland had already been descended in rafts, the risks appeared to be justifiable, and four rafts were built. Mr. Staniforth Smith started out first with three police and two carriers, and Mr. Bell and Mr. Pratt arranged to follow in quick succession with the rest. In two hundred yards the first raft was upset, but its occupants managed to hang on. Instead of the rapids disappearing they grew worse, and after four or five wild miles the party dashed into a timber block. One of the natives was so seriously injured that he died next morning. Mr. Staniforth Smith then started to go back along the river, in the hope of joining his companions, but found that he was on an island with swift streams on either side. Next morning the party tried to ford the river, and with some difficulty succeeded. As they were cutting a track up a bank they met two of

New Guinea Pygmies contrasted with ordinary Natives.
(By permission of Messrs. Seeley, Service, & Co.)

the police, who had lost their rifles, and who informed them that Mr. Bell and Mr. Pratt were on the other bank of the river, and that several of the carriers had been drowned. The party had now been two days without food, so Mr. Staniforth Smith resolved to turn and travel down the stream in the hope of finding smoother water and a native village. They had no means of making a fire, and in any case there were no sago or bread-fruit trees in the neighbourhood.

For five and a half days the explorers hacked their way downstream. During all that time they had no food of any kind, and no shelter from torrential rains except a few palm leaves. On the sixth day, after travelling twenty miles, they saw natives on the opposite bank. They built a rough raft and managed to cross. It was just in time, for they were now utterly exhausted; but the food which the natives gave them revived them. Curiously enough, as they were at their meal the party of Mr. Bell and Mr. Pratt came out of the jungle. They had, if possible, suffered even worse disasters. Both the white men, though powerful swimmers, had been nearly drowned, and seven of the carriers had lost their lives. They would certainly have perished had they not had the luck the day before to shoot a wild pig.

By this time it was clear that whatever stream they were on it was not the Strickland, for the Strickland flowed south-west, and this river ran nearly due east. The natives, who had never seen a white man before, took them to their village and treated them kindly. The good repute of the British official throughout the wilds now stood them in good stead. They hoped that the river would soon be clear of rapids; but to their consternation there was nothing but gorges and whirlpools for another hundred miles. The stream was the Kikor in its middle reaches, the same stream as they had ascended from the coast. It took them twenty-nine days to pass the hundred miles of gorges, and during that time they rarely had a full meal. On one occasion the whole party worked for seven days without getting anything to eat except a few handfuls of soup-powder and a few tins of cocoa, saved from the capsized rafts. They had no matches, so they had to keep a fire burning day and night. They slept in caves and under palm leaves, which made no pretence of keeping out the rain.

By the twenty-ninth day the river seemed smooth enough for rafts, and the explorers again embarked, and managed to cover fifty miles without any serious misadventure. But next day the rapids began again, and their two canoes, made of hollow logs, were upset. They descended the rapids for ten miles, hanging on to the upturned logs, before they could land. That night they spent in the rain, without food ; and starting again at daybreak, they suddenly saw, to their immense relief, European tents, and were welcomed by an officer of the constabulary, who had been sent out to look for them. They had reached the exact spot from which they had struck north to Mount Murray at the beginning of their journey! When, two days later, they arrived at the coast, they had travelled in fifteen weeks approximately 524 miles through utterly unknown country—374 miles on foot and 150 by river.

Mr. Staniforth Smith encountered every misfortune that can meet the traveller except one—he had no trouble with the natives. Indeed, by his tact and patience he made friends everywhere with the bushmen, and the survivors of the party owed to them their lives. By some strange system of bush telegraphy the repute of the white men was spread from village to village. It was the one piece of good fortune that befell the explorers, and it was final in its effect, for it made the difference between life and death. I do not know any narrative of exploration which contains adventures more desperate than those whirling voyages on upturned rafts through black ravines ; or that month when starving men hacked their way through the jungle along the torrent's bank in a perpetual tempest of rain.*

* For this journey Mr. Staniforth Smith received in 1923 the gold medal of the Royal Geographical Society.

IX

MOUNT EVEREST

MOUNT EVEREST

(*Map*, p. 272.)

I

THE Himalaya not only contain the loftiest peaks on the globe, but can boast at least eighty summits loftier than those of any other range. The Andes come next, but their highest point, Aconcagua, is only 23,060 feet. In the huge mountain land which bounds India on the north, and which stretches as great a distance as from the English Channel to the Caspian, there are more than eighty peaks above 24,000 feet, some twenty above 26,000, and six above 27,000. Mount Everest, the highest, is, according to the latest measurements, 29,140 feet high. Its true character was not always recognized. At one time Chimborazo, in the Andes, was thought to "outsoar Himalay." In the middle of last century Kanchenjunga, which fills the eye of the traveller who looks north from Darjeeling, was believed to be the loftiest of the world's mountains. At that time officers of

the Indian Government were conducting the great
Trigonometrical Survey, during which they discovered
a summit for which they could find no native name,
and which they labelled Peak XV. In 1852, when the
observations had been worked out, an official rushed
breathlessly into the room of the Surveyor-General
in Calcutta with the news that Peak XV. proved to
be 29,002 feet high, and was therefore the chief
mountain in the world. As its native name was
unknown, it was called after Sir George Everest,
who had been in charge of the survey. The name is
beautiful in itself, and may well stand; though, had
the circumstances been otherwise, there would have
been much to be said for the Tibetan name, " Chomo-
lungmo," which means " Goddess Mother of the
Mountains."

The ascent of Everest was a project which only
slowly entered into men's minds. When the great
peak was first discovered mountaineering was still in
its infancy, and for a generation afterwards climbers
were preoccupied with the Alps. Then mountaineers
began to look farther afield, and first the Caucasus
and then the Andes were conquered, till some thirty
years ago the ambitious began to turn their eyes to
the Himalaya. Gradually the limit of achievement

on high snows was extended. On Trisul, Dr. Long-
staff in ten and a half hours ascended from 17,450 feet
to the summit of 23,360 feet. On Kamet, Mr. Charles
Meade took coolies up to a camp of 23,600 feet. The
Duke of the Abruzzi, after his ascent of Ruwenzori,
attacked, with a splendidly equipped party, K^2, that
icy lump in the Karakoram, the second highest of
the world's mountains, and reached a height of 24,600
feet, which, till the year 1921, remained the world's
record. In 1920 Dr. Kellas found that on reasonable
snow he could ascend at a rate of 600 feet an hour
above 21,000 feet. It was inevitable that, when the
Great War was over, lovers of high places should fix
their thoughts on Everest.

It had long been a dream of mountaineers. Lord
Curzon, when Viceroy of India, had suggested the
exploration of Everest to the Royal Geographical
Society and the Alpine Club. But there were political
difficulties connected with the journey through Tibet
or Nepal, and even a reconnaissance of the mountain
proved impossible. Cecil Rawling (who fell at the
Third Battle of Ypres as a Brigadier-General with the
21st Division), during his journey in 1904 to the head
waters of the Brahmaputra, saw for the first time,
from a distance of sixty miles, the north side of

Everest, and believed that it might be climbed. I well remember how in the year before the war he and I planned an expedition which was to cover two seasons, and explore that northern side. In March, 1919, Captain Noel urged the Royal Geographical Society to undertake the work, and Sir Francis Younghusband, the President of the Society in the following year, in conjunction with the Alpine Club, entered into negotiations with the Government of India. Permission was obtained from the Tibetan authorities, and in January 1921 a Joint Committee of the Royal Geographical Society and the Alpine Club proceeded to organize an expedition.

There were many to ask what was the use of such an enterprise, which would be costly, difficult, and certainly dangerous. The answer is that it was no earthly use, and that in that lay its supreme merit. The war had called forth the finest qualities of human nature, and with the advent of peace there seemed a risk of the world slipping back into a dull material- ism. Men had begun to ask of everything its cash value, and to cherish, as if it were a virtue, a narrow utilitarian commonsense. To embark upon some- thing which had no material value was a vindication of the essential idealism of the human spirit. In Sir

Francis Younghusband's words, " The sight of climbers struggling upwards to the supreme pinnacle would have taught men to lift their eyes to the hills—to raise them off the ground and divert them, if only for a moment, to something pure and lofty and satisfying to that inner craving for the worthiest which all men have hidden in their souls. And when they see men thrown back at first, but returning again and again to the assault, till, with faltering footsteps and gasping breaths, they at last reach the summit, they will thrill with pride. They will no longer be obsessed with the thought of what mites they are in comparison with the mountains—how insignificant they are beside their material surroundings. They will have a proper pride in themselves, and a well-grounded faith in the capacity of spirit to dominate material."

These are almost the words of Theophile Gautier's defence of mountaineers : " Ils sont la volonté protestante contre l'obstacle aveugle, et ils plantent sur l'inaccessible le drapeau de l'intelligence humaine." If the climber wants a further statement of his creed let it be that of Mr. Belloc, when he first saw the Alps from the ridge of the Jura. " Up there, the sky above and below them, the great peaks made communion between that homing, creeping part of me which loves vineyards, and dances, and a slow movement among pastures, and that other part which is only properly at home in Heaven. . . . These, the great Alps, seen thus, link one in some way to one's immortality. Nor is it possible to convey, or even to suggest, these few fifty miles and these few thousand feet; there is something more. Let me put it thus : that from the height of Weissenstein I saw, as it were, my religion. I mean humility, the fear of death, the terror of height or of distance, the glory of God, the infinite potentiality of reception, whence springs that divine thirst of the soul ; my aspiration also towards completion and my confidence in the dual destiny. For I know that we laughers have a gross cousinship with the most high, and it is this constant and perpetual quarrel which feeds the spring of merriment in the soul of a sane man. Since I could now see such a wonder, and it could work such things in my mind, therefore some day I should be part of it. That is what I feel. That it is also which leads some men to climb mountain-tops, but not me, for I am afraid of slipping down." *

And now for the great mountain itself. First of all, it is a rock peak. All the upper part is a great

* *The Path to Rome.*

pyramid of stone, with three main *arêtes*—the West, the South-West, and the North-East. It lies exactly on the frontier between Tibet and Nepal, and from the Nepalese side and the plains of India it is hard to get a good view of it, for only a wedge of white is seen peeping between and over other peaks. On the Tibetan side, however, it stands clear, and its pre-eminence over its neighbours is patent. Now, in all attacks upon a great peak the first question is how to get to it—a problem most difficult in the case of other Himalayan summits like K^2, and of peaks like Mount McKinley in Alaska and Mount Robson in Canada. It is not only the question of the climbers getting there, but of transporting the food and tents and accessories required by a well-equipped expedition. Had the only route to Everest lain through the deep-cut gorges of Nepal, the transport problem might have been insuperable. But here came in the value of Tibet, which is a high plateau, averaging twelve or thirteen thousand feet. It was possible to take a large party, with baggage animals, up through the passes of Sikkim to the Kampa Dzong (Kampa Jong), and then westwards along the north side of the range to a base camp at Tingri Dzong, due north of the mountain. Everest itself would be forty or fifty

miles from such a base camp, but there was a clear
road to it by the upper glens and glaciers of the
Arun, which flows north and east before it turns south
and cuts its way through the Himalayan wall.

The problem of access to the base was, therefore,
not a hard one. The problem of the ascent was two-
fold—part physiological, part physical. Could human
beings survive at an altitude of 29,000 feet—human
beings who were forced to carry loads and to move
their limbs? Aviators, of course, had risen to greater
heights, but they had not been compelled to exert
themselves. Could a man in action support life in
that rarified air? Above 20,000 feet a cubic foot of
air contains less than half the oxygen which it holds
at sea-level. As the working of the body depends
upon the oxygen supplied through the lungs, this
fact was bound to lessen enormously man's physical
energy. On the other hand, it had been found that
the human frame could adapt itself to great altitudes
by increasing the number of red blood corpuscles.
Dr. Kellas had been able to climb 600 feet an hour
above 21,000 feet, and Mr. Meade had camped in
comparative comfort at 23,600 feet. Still, the highest
altitude yet reached had been only 24,600 feet, and
no one could say what difference the extra 4,500 feet

might make. Clearly, before the final climbing began
it would be necessary to acclimatize the party. In
the last resort oxygen might be artificially supplied
to the climbers. The physiological problem was of
the kind which could only be solved in practice.

The second was the physical. A man might live
and even move slowly above, say, 26,000 feet, but it
was quite certain that no human being would be
capable of the severe exertions required by difficult
climbing. If the last stage of Everest proved to be
like the last stages of many Himalayan mountains,
then the thing was strictly impossible. The hope
was that on the Tibetan side the *arêtes* might be
easy going. It all depended upon finding an easy
route, and being able to make an ultimate camp at
some point like 26,000 feet. There was good hope
that the first might be possible, judging from Rawling's survey at a distance of sixty miles and the known
geographical features of the Tibetan side of the range.
The other physical difficulties would be the gigantic
scale of Himalayan obstacles, the hugeness of the
ice-fields and glaciers, the immensity of the rock-falls
and avalanches. Also at a great height there would
be the bitter cold to lower vitality, and the likelihood
of violent winds. Much would depend on the weather,

which was still an unknown quantity. Indeed, all the physical factors were in the region of speculation ; only a reconnaissance could determine them. It might be that the expedition would have to turn back at once, confessing its task impossible.

General Bruce, who was the chief living authority on Himalayan travelling, was unable to accompany the party, so Colonel Howard-Bury was selected as leader. An elaborate scientific equipment was prepared, and steps were taken to get the full scientific value out of the journey. But the primary object was mountaineering : first a reconnaissance, and then, if fortune favoured, an effort to reach the summit. The four climbers chosen were Mr. Harold Raeburn, who, in 1920, had done good work on the spurs of Kanchenjunga ; Dr. Kellas, who had reached 23,400 feet on Kamet ; and two younger men, Mr. George Leigh Mallory and Mr. Bullock, distinguished members of the Alpine Club, who had been together at Winchester. In India they were to be joined by Major Morshead and Major Wheeler, of the Indian Survey. Early in May 1921, the party assembled at Darjeeling.

II

The start from Darjeeling was on 18th May. The first stage through Sikkim, and by way of the Chumbi valley to the Tibetan plateau, was over familiar ground, which need not be described. There was a good deal of trouble with the mules, which had been badly chosen, but no incident of importance happened till Dochen was reached, the point where their road left the main road to Lhasa. At Kampa Dzong, Dr. Kellas died suddenly from heart failure—an irreparable loss to the expedition, for he had been one of the mountaineers from whom most was looked for, and he was the only member of the party qualified by his medical knowledge to carry out experiments in oxygen and blood pressure. There, too, Mr. Raeburn fell sick, and had to return to Sikkim.

The expedition made its way almost due west behind the main chain of the Himalaya, until one evening its members saw, almost due south of them, a beautiful peak which was apparently very high. The natives called it Chomo-Uri, which means the " Goddess of the Turquoise Peak," and from observations next morning it was clear that it was Everest. They passed some wonderful monasteries perching on the face of perpendicular crags, and eventually, on 19th June, they reached Tingri Dzong, after a month's travelling from Darjeeling. This was the spot they had decided upon for their base camp.

The obvious route to Everest seemed to be by way of the Rongbuk valley, where the great Rongbuk Glacier flowed from its northern face. There, accordingly, the two climbers, Mr. Mallory and Mr. Bullock, established themselves. The preliminary reconnaissance, however, proved to be a somewhat intricate matter. It was soon plain that there were no easy approaches from the west, so Colonel Howard-Bury moved his headquarters to Kharta, on the east side, close to the Arun. That river, which there is about one hundred yards wide, a little farther down enters great gorges, in which, within a course of twenty miles, it drops from 12,000 feet to 7,500 feet, or over 200 feet in a mile—a far more wonderful spectacle than anything on the Brahmaputra.

On 2nd August, Mr. Mallory and Mr. Bullock started their exploration of the eastern approaches to the mountain. This was no easy business, for the valleys were separated by ridges, the lowest point of which was higher than any mountain in Europe, and every route had to be explored personally, for no information could be had from the natives. The two main valleys running down on the east side of Everest are the Kharta and, farther south, the Kama. The latter valley was first explored, and it was found that it ended under the precipitous eastern face of the mountain, and that there was no way from it of reaching the North-East ridge. It was a marvellous valley for scenery, but for mountaineering impracticable.

A move was accordingly made to the Kharta valley to the north. Mr. Mallory and Mr. Bullock proceeded up this till they reached the glacier of the Kharta River, and at last found a valley which seemed to lead them straight to the North-East ridge. It was now, however, early August, the monsoon was blowing, and everywhere there was deep, soft, fresh snow. They returned accordingly to the camp at Kharta to wait till weather conditions became better.

What was called the Advance Base Camp was established in the Kharta valley at a height of 17,350 feet, in a grassy hollow well sheltered from the wind, and amid a glory of Alpine flowers. Meantime Mr. Mallory and Mr. Bullock spent their time in carrying wood and stores to a camp higher up the valley. This was finally established at a height of some 20,000 feet, well up the Kharta Glacier. At the glacier head was a pass called the Lhakpa La, or "Windy Gap," and the next step was to form a camp there at a height of 22,350 feet. It was in this neighbourhood that the tracks, probably of a wolf, were found, which the coolies attributed to the "Wild Men of the Snows."

From the Lhakpa La the mountaineers were now looking straight at Everest, and at last were able to unriddle its tangled topography. The attention of the reader is called to the map. It will be seen that the great Rongbuk Glacier, which descends from the western side of the northern face, receives as a feeder the East Rongbuk Glacier. The entrance to the latter is so small that Mr. Mallory and Mr. Bullock had failed to notice it in their exploration of the main glacier. This lesser Rongbuk Glacier ends on the eastern part of the northern face of the mountain, and between its head and that of the main glacier is the pass called the Chang La, or North Col. From the Lhakpa La one looks into the East Rongbuk Glacier with the North Col straight in front. If the North Col could be attained, it seemed to the mountaineers to be possible, by working up the easy northern face, to attain the North-East ridge at a point above the main difficulties.

The camp on the Lhakpa La was not a comfortable

place, with a howling wind, 34 degrees of frost, and
little stuffy tents which gave dubious protection and
inevitable headaches. It was decided that the two
expert Alpine climbers, with a few picked coolies,
should alone attempt the North Col, and, if fortune
favoured, prospect the farther route, while the others
returned to the 20,000-feet camp.

We are now concerned with the doings only of Mr.
Mallory and Mr. Bullock, who were to attempt the
North Col. In the weeks since their arrival in the
neighbourhood of Everest they had been studying
its contours with the eyes of trained mountaineers.
They saw that it was a great rock mass, " coated often
with a thin layer of white powder, which is blown
about its sides, and bearing perennial snow only
on the gentler ledges and on several wide faces less
steep than the rest." They saw that from the point
of the North-East shoulder a more or less broad *arête*
fell northward to the snow col called the Chang La. If
they could reach that snow col the road to the North-
East ridge looked reasonably simple. They had seen
that the Chang La would be very difficult of attainment from the Rongbuk Glacier, and that was why
they had turned their minds to an eastern approach.
Here is their conclusion, in Mr. Mallory's words,

reached about the third week in July : "If ever the mountain were to be climbed, the way would not lie along the whole length of any one of its colossal ridges. Progress could only be made along comparatively easy ground, and anything like a prolonged sharp crest or a series of towers would inevitably bar the way, simply by the time it would require to overcome such obstacles. But the North *arête*, coming down to the gap between Everest and the North Peak, Changtse, is not of this character. From the horizontal structure of the mountain there is no excrescence of rock pinnacles in this part, and the steep walls of rock which run across the north face are merged with it before they reach this part, which is comparatively smooth and continuous, a bluntly rounded edge. . . . The great question before us now was to be one of access. Could the North Col be reached from the east, and how could we attain this point ? "

We have seen the two climbers as far on their journey as the Lhakpa La, looking over the East Rongbuk Glacier to the North Col. The chief difficulty, it was soon evident, would be the wall under the col, which must be over 500 feet high, and appeared to be very steep.

On the morning of 23rd September, Mr. Mallory, Mr.
Bullock, and Mr. Wheeler started from the camp on
the Lhakpa La with ten coolies, some of whom were
mountain-sick, and all of whom were affected by the
height. They started late, and resolved to make an
easy day, pitching their tents that night in the open
snow under the North Col. They had looked for a
sheltered camp, but the place proved to be a temple
of the winds, and no one that night had much sleep.
Next morning, the 24th, a few hours after sunrise,
they began to climb the slopes under the wall, and
found them easier than they had feared. By 11.30
the party was on the col. Only three coolies had
accompanied them, two of whom were already very
tired. Of the three sahibs, only Mr. Mallory was in
anything like good condition. The place was scourged
by icy blasts, and frequently in a whirl of powdery
snow, but there could be no doubt that the *arête* in
front of them was accessible. In that gale, however,
they dare not attempt it, so they struggled back to
their camp below the wall. Next morning, the 25th,
a council of war was held. It was clear that they
must either go on or go back. In their plan they
had dreamed of making a camp at 26,000 feet, but
that was now out of the question. It was too late

in the season, the weather was too bad, and the party
was too weak. There was nothing for it but to return,
and accordingly they struggled over the Lhakpa La,
back to the Kharta valley and the road to England.

The reconnaissance of 1921 had established certain
facts of the first importance. The first was as to the
proper season for the attempt. The rainfall in the
Himalaya that year was abnormal, and the monsoon
began and finished later than usual. But it was clear
that between its end and the coming of winter there
was not sufficient time to give the climbers a chance
of good weather. The next attempt must obviously
be made before the coming of the monsoon—that is,
in May or June. The second fact established was
the best way of attempting the summit. The only
feasible route lay from the Chang La up the subsidiary
ridge to the shoulder of the North-East *arête*. The
distance from the Chang La to the top was not more
than two miles, and the rise not more than 6,000
feet. So far as the climbers on the pass could judge
—and their conclusion was supported by numerous
photographs from other points—there seemed to be
no very great difficulties on this route in the shape
of steep rocks. It looked as if it might be practicable

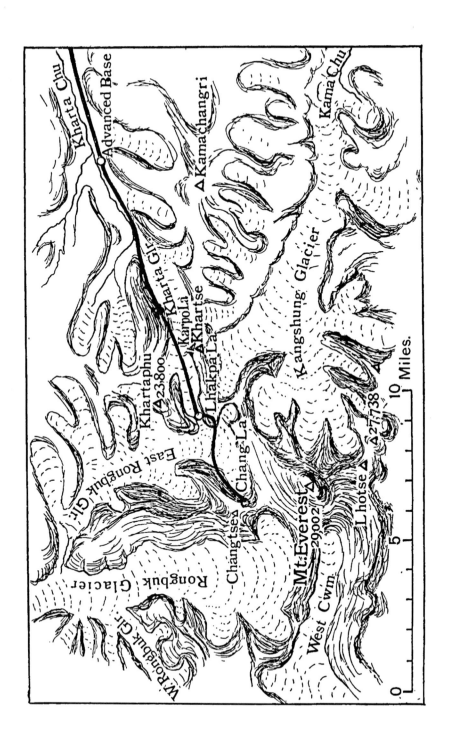

to find a site for a camp at about 26,000 feet. By this route the North-East *arête* would be reached at about 28,000 feet. The thousand feet from that point to the summit looked slightly more difficult, and appeared to possess certain rock towers, which, however, might be circumvented. The actual top seemed to be a cap of snow with a steep blunt edge on the side of the ridge.

The transport question must always be difficult. The thousand feet from the East Rongbuk Glacier to the Chang La, half of which was very steep, might give trouble to laden coolies, especially earlier in the season when the ice was uncovered by snow. An advanced base camp on the Chang La would, of course, be essential if a high camp were to be made at 26,000 feet. But the physical problem might be regarded as solved—at any rate as far as the shoulder of the North-East *arête*. On the physiological question little light had been thrown. The climbers in September 1921 were all more or less tired from spending long periods in high camps, and could not be regarded as at the top of their form. Yet in the case of most members of the party the process of acclimatization had been rapid, and Mr. Mallory on the Chang La was remarkably fit. What would happen, however, at the higher altitudes ? The effect of these upon the human body had not been decided.

The conclusion from the year's work was that while no insuperable difficulty had been proved in the problem, yet for success there must be a combination of happy chances in the shape of weather, the condition of the snow, the endurance of the transport coolies, and the bodily fitness of the climbers. A second attempt would be justified, but it could not be regarded with anything like confidence. The enterprise was seriously and responsibly envisaged, and no better expression of the spirit of those who undertook it can be found than in Mr. Mallory's own words : "It might be possible for two men to struggle somehow to the summit, disregarding every other consideration. It is a different matter to climb the mountain as mountaineers would have it climbed. Principles, time-honoured in the Alpine Club, must, of course, be respected in the ascent of Mount Everest. The party must keep a margin of safety. It is not to be a mad enterprise, rashly pushed on regardless of danger. The ill-considered acceptance of any and every risk has no part in the essence of persevering courage. A mountaineering enterprise may keep sanity and sound judgment, and remain an adventure.

And of all principles to which we hold, the first is
that of mutual help. What is to be done for a man
who is sick or abnormally exhausted at these high
altitudes ? His companions must see to it that he
is taken down at the first opportunity, and with an
adequate escort ; and the obligation is the same
whether he be sahib or coolie. If we ask a man to
carry our loads up the mountain, we must care for
his welfare at need."

III

The 1922 party had as its leader Brigadier-General
the Hon. C. G. Bruce, the supreme authority upon the
Himalaya, to the exploration of which he had devoted
much of his life. He knew the hill people, too, as
no other man knew them, and his advice was invaluable in the selection of porters. The climbers were
Mr. Mallory, Mr. Finch (who had been selected for
the expedition of the year before, but had been unable
to accompany it), Mr. Norton, and Mr. Somervell—all
of whom were trained mountaineers ; and Captain
Geoffrey Bruce, who had never done any serious
climbing before. Major Morshead was also of the
party. The 1921 expedition had discovered what

seemed a possible route to the summit by the North Col, and the new expedition proposed to follow its tracks. It was stronger in *personnel* than its predecessor, and much stronger in equipment, for it had learned many lessons from the experiences of the year before. Among other things, it carried a supply of oxygen in bottles, and the necessary apparatus to use it.

The party, being resolved to make the attempt before the monsoon broke, made straight for the old advanced base camp in the Kharta valley. Thanks to General Bruce's consummate skill in the organization of mountain travel, it reached that point on the date fixed and with everybody in good health. The next duty was to establish an advanced camp one stage before the North Col, up to which porters could be brought without undue fatigue. The summit of the Lhakpa La was abandoned, and an advanced base, known as Camp No. 3, was established under the west side of the pass, close to the East Rongbuk Glacier.

The next step was to ascertain whether the road to the North Col was practicable, for when Mr. Mallory's party had travelled it the year before there had been fresh snow, and at this early season there was a danger of bare ice. Mr. Somervell and Mr. Mallory, on 13th

May, with one coolie, set forth from Camp No. 3 on a reconnaissance, and found that the route they had followed the year before was one sheet of glittering ice. They saw, however, that they could cut their way into a corridor filled with good snow, which would lead them up to the foot of the final slope, and that final slope proved also to be snow and not ice. On the North Col they found a difficulty they had not looked for. Between the point at which they reached it and Everest itself was an ice cliff, which the year before they had circumvented. Now they found their way barred by a hopeless crevasse. Ultimately they discovered a route at the far end of the ice cliff, and reached the level snow from which the north ridge of Everest springs.

The next few days were occupied in bringing up supplies to Camp 4 on the North Col. They had only nine porters available, and this decided them that it would not be feasible to make two camps on the face of the mountain. They resolved to attempt to make one camp at about 26,000 feet, and from that to make their final effort.

On the 19th the four climbers, Mr. Mallory, Mr. Norton, Major Morshead, and Mr. Somervell, left Camp 3 at a quarter to nine in the morning, and an hour after midday were busy putting up tents and arranging stores at Camp 4 on the North Col. The sun set at 4.30, and they turned in for the night in the best of spirits. On the morrow they proposed to carry up two of the small tents, two double sleeping-sacks, food for a day and a half, cooking-pots, and two thermos flasks. They would make four loads of the stuff, which would give two porters to each load, with a man to spare.

On 20th May, Mr. Mallory got up at 5 a.m., and found that there was no sign of life in the tents in which the nine porters were quartered. The coolies had shut themselves in so hermetically that they were all unwell, and four of them were suffering badly from mountain-sickness. Only five were able to embark on the day's work. Breakfast was a slow business, because everything was frozen hard, and the dish of spaghetti which they had promised themselves could only be prepared after an elaborate process of thawing.

A start was made at 7 a.m., and everything went smoothly at first, for ropes had been fixed between their camp and the col itself, so as to help them on their return. From the col a broad snow ridge went up at an easy angle, and all the climbers felt that bodily fitness which is the assurance of success.

Then their troubles began. The first was the cold. The sun had no more warmth in it than a candle, and a bitter wind began to blow from the west. They came to an end of the ridge of stones on which they had been progressing easily, and realized that they must get some shelter from the wind by moving to the east side of the shoulder. Step-cutting was now necessary, and at that height the exertion required was extraordinarily severe. Moreover, the cold was telling upon them, and the porters especially suffered badly. After some 300 feet of steps they rested about noon under the shelter of some rocks at 25,000 feet.

It seemed to them that they could not get their loads much higher, and that they had better look out for a camp, for the porters had to return to the North Col. But a camping ground was not easy to find. At last, on the east side of the ridge, they discovered a steep slab, up to which they could level the ground. It was a poor place, for the incline was sharp, most of the floor was composed of broken rocks, and men lying down would inevitably slip on top of each other. There, however, they placed the little tents, each with its double sleeping-bag, and melted snow for their makeshift supper. The porters started back for the North Col, and the climbers, two in each bed, did their best to keep warm. All four had suffered a good deal from the cold. Mr. Norton's ear was badly swollen, three of Mr. Mallory's fingers were touched with the frost, and Major Morshead was chilled to the bone and clearly unwell.

The wind dropped in the evening, and during the night fresh snow fell. At 6.50 on the morning of 21st May they crawled from their sleeping-bags and made a laborious and exiguous breakfast, for only one thermos flask had turned up. At eight o'clock they started, none of them feeling their best after the stuffy, headachy night. Major Morshead was unable to go with them, for his illness had increased, and most regretfully the other three went on without him.

A good deal of fresh snow had fallen, but the first hours of climbing were not very difficult. The worst trouble was the perverse stratification of the mountain, for all the ledges tilted the wrong way. Slowly they crawled up, first regaining the ridge by turning west, and then following the ridge itself in the direction of the point of the North-East arête. They decided that they must turn back at about two o'clock if they were to make the descent in reasonable safety. Besides, they had to consider Major Morshead left alone in Camp 5.

At 2.15 they reached the head of the rocks, about 500 feet below the point where the north shoulder joined the North-East *arête*. Here they had a clear view of the summit. The aneroid gave the elevation as 26,800 feet, but it is possible that it may have been nearly 200 feet more. Their advance had for some time been reduced to a very slow crawl, but none of the party were really exhausted. It was wise, however, to turn while they had sufficient strength to get back to Camp 4. They tried moving westward, where there seemed to be more snow, but they found that the snow slopes were a series of slabs with an ugly tilt under a thin covering of new snow ; so they went back to the ridge and followed their old tracks. At four o'clock they reached Camp 5, and picked up Major Morshead and their tents and sleeping-bags. After that the going became more difficult, as the fresh-fallen snow had made even easy ground treacherous. One slip did occur, and the three men were held only by the rope secured round Mr. Mallory's ice axe.

The descent now became a race with the fast-gathering darkness. When they got to the snow ridge they could find no trace of the steps they had made the day before, and had to cut them over again. At this point they were in sight of the watchers far below at Camp 3 on the glacier. Major Morshead was suffering severely and could only move a few steps at a time. As the night drew in, lightning began to flicker from the clouds in the west, but happily the wind did not rise. They were soon at the crevasses and the ice cliff, and, as the air was calm, it was possible to light a lantern to guide them. They hunted desperately to find the fixed rope, which would take them down to the terrace, where they could see their five tents awaiting them, but the rope was covered with snow, and at that moment the lantern gave out. Happily somebody hooked up the buried rope, and after that it was plain going to the tents.

They reached them at 11.30, and could find no fuel or cooking-pots. Their mouths were parched with thirst, and the best beverage they could concoct was a mixture of jam and snow with frozen condensed milk. Mr. Mallory ascribes to the influence of this stuff "the uncontrollable shudderings, spasms of muscular contraction in belly and back, which I suffered in my sleeping-bag, and which caused me to sit up and inhale again great whiffs from the night air, as though the habit of deep breathing had settled upon me indispensably."

The four men did not waste time next morning on

the North Col, for they were tormented by thirst and hunger. It took them six hours to reach Camp 3, for they had to make a staircase beneath the new snow which the porters could use, in order to fetch down their baggage, since they did not intend to spend the night at Camp 3 . without their sleeping-bags. At midday they were back in comparative comfort, with certain solid conclusions as the result of the venture. One was as to the difficulties of new snow and the precariousness of the weather ; another was as to the unexpected capacity of the porters. But the most important was as to the need of oxygen. They had reached a point very little below 27,000 feet, and that left 2,000 feet to be surmounted before the summit was reached. For success, a higher camp was needed than Camp 5, and the men who started from it must, if possible, have an extra stimulus to counteract the malign effects of altitude. If Everest chose to clothe itself with air containing less oxygen than a man needed, the defect must be supplied. If a climber used extra clothes to counteract the cold, he must use some extra device to supplement the atmosphere.

IV

We come now to the second attempt of 1922, in which oxygen was used. Certain eminent scientists at home had held that Everest could never be conquered without its aid, and the expedition had brought a very full equipment—oxygen stored in light steel cylinders, and a somewhat complex apparatus for its use. There had been oxygen drill parades among the party, and perhaps it might have been well had they used it straight away for one main attempt, instead of making the first effort without it. Unfortunately the apparatus needed overhauling, and it was not till 22nd May, when Mr. Mallory and his party were coming down from the mountain, that four sets were ready for use. As to the legitimacy of such a device in mountaineering, Mr. Finch's arguments are final.

" Few of us, I think, who stop to ponder for a brief second, will deny that our very existence in this enlightened twentieth century, with all its amenities of modern civilization is . . . ' artificial.' Most of us have learned to respect progress, and to appreciate the meaning and advantages of adaptability. For instance, it is a fairly firmly established fact that warmth is necessary to life. The mountaineer, acting on this knowledge, conserves, as far as possible, his animal heat by wearing especially warm clothing. No one demurs ; it is the commonsense thing to do. He pours his hot tea from a thermos bottle—and never blushes ! Nonchalantly, without fear of adverse criticism, he doctors up his insides with special heat- and energy-giving foods and stimulants ! From the sun's ultra-violet rays and the wind's bitter cold he boldly dares to protect his eyes with Crookes' anti-glare glasses. Further, he wears boots that to the average layman look ridiculous ! The use of caffeine, to supply just a little more buck to an almost worn-out frame, is not cavilled at, despite its being a synthetic drug, the manufacture of which involves the employment of complicated plant and methods. If science could prepare oxygen in tabloid form, or supply it to us in thermos flasks that we might imbibe it like our hot tea, the stigma of ' artificiality ' would, perhaps, be effectually removed. But when it has to be carried in special containers, its whole essence is held to be altered, and, by using it, the mountaineer is taking a sneaking, unfair advantage of the mountain ! In answer to this grave charge, I would remind the accuser that, by the inhalation of a little life-giving gas, the climber does not smooth away the rough rocks of the mountain, or still the storm ; nor is he an Aladdin who, by a rub on a magic ring, is wafted by invisible agents to his goal. Oxygen renders available more of his store of energy, and so hastens his steps, but it does not, alas ! fit the wings of Mercury to his feet. The logic of the anti-oxygenist is surely faulty."

On 20th May, Mr. Finch and Captain Geoffrey Bruce arrived at Camp 3, accompanied by Tejbir, one of the four Gurkha non-commissioned officers lent to the expedition. There they found the oxygen apparatus in bad condition, and had to tinker at it for four days. During this period they made a trial trip to Camp 4 on the North Col, using oxygen. A good deal of new step-cutting had to be done, for fresh snow had fallen, but in spite of that, the oxygen enabled them to get to the col in three hours and to return in fifty minutes, with halts to take three dozen photographs.

On 24th May, Mr. Finch, Captain Bruce, Captain Noel, the official photographer, and Tejbir, with twelve porters, went up to the North Col and camped for the night. Next morning, the 25th, brought a clear, windy sky, and at eight o'clock the twelve porters, with the camp outfit, provisions for one day, and the oxygen cylinders, started up the North ridge, followed an hour and a half later by Mr. Finch, Captain

Bruce, and Tejbir, each carrying a load of over thirty pounds. All fifteen used oxygen. It was their intention to make a camp above 26,000 feet; but after one o'clock the wind freshened and snow began, so it was deemed advisable, in order to ensure the safe return of the porters to the North Col, to camp at 25,500 feet. The camping place was no better than that which Mr. Mallory had found; the place was on the actual crest of the ridge, for the west side was scourged by wind, and there was no good position on the east side. The tent was pitched on a little platform on the edge of precipices falling to the East Rongbuk Glacier, 4,000 feet below. The tent was secured as well as possible by guy-ropes; but when the climbers got into their sleeping-bags it was both blowing and snowing hard, and minute flakes filled the tent. Snow was melted, and a tepid meal was cooked—a really warm meal was out of the question, for at that altitude water boils at so low a temperature that a man can hold his hand in it without discomfort.

As the night closed in, the two climbers comforted themselves with the assurance that next day they would get to the top. But after sunset the wind increased to a gale so furious that even the ground sheet with the three men lying on it was lifted completely off the earth. They blocked up the small openings as well as they could, but before midnight everything inside was covered with spindrift. It was impossible to sleep. They had to be constantly on the watch to prevent the flaps being torn open and to hold the tent down ; for they realized that if once the gale got hold of their shelter the whole outfit would be blown on to the glacier below.

Few adventurers have ever spent a more awful night. Tejbir had all the placidity of his race, and Captain Bruce, who was making his first serious mountaineering expedition on the highest of the world's mountains, was as cheerful as if he had been sleeping in an ordinary Alpine *cabane*. Here is Mr. Finch's own description :—

" By one o'clock on the morning of the 26th the gale reached its maximum. The wild flapping of the canvas made a noise like that of machine-gun fire. So deafening was it that we could scarcely hear each other speak. Later there came interludes of comparative lull, succeeded by bursts of storm more furious than ever. During such lulls we took it in turn to go outside to tighten up slackened guy-ropes, and also succeeded in tying down the tent more firmly with our Alpine rope. It was impossible to work in the open for more than three or four minutes at a stretch, so profound was the exhaustion induced by this brief exposure to the fierce cold wind."

Morning broke with no lull in the violence of the elements. They prepared a make-shift meal, and spent the forenoon hours in desperate anxiety. At midday the storm seemed to reach the summit of its fury, and matters were made more awkward by a stone cutting a great hole in the tent. Mercifully an hour later the wind suddenly dropped, and the anxious occupants of the tent could prospect the weather.

The sensible thing would have been to make a retreat to the North Col, but there was no thought of giving up. The party were unanimous in resolving to hang on and make the attempt the following day. With the last of their fuel they cooked supper—a frugal meal, for, since they had only carried provisions for one day, they were now on very short rations. As they settled down for the night voices were heard outside, and the porters from the North Col appeared, bringing thermos flasks of hot beef-tea and tea, sent by Captain Noel. In a little more comfort they tried to sleep. All three, however, were strained and weak from their labours of the past twenty-four hours, and they felt a numbing cold creeping up their limbs. Mr. Finch had the happy inspiration to use oxygen, and so arranged the apparatus that each could breathe a small quantity throughout the night. " The result was marvellous. We slept well and warmly. Whenever the tube delivering the gas fell out of Bruce's mouth as he slept, I could see him stir uneasily in the eerie greenish light of the moon as it filtered through the canvas. Then, half unconsciously replacing the tube, he would fall once more into a peaceful slumber."

Next morning, the 27th, they woke well and hungry, and after a struggle with their boots, which were frozen stiff, started off at 6.30, Captain Bruce and Mr. Finch carrying each over forty pounds, and Tejbir some fifty pounds. Their plan was to take Tejbir as far as the North-East shoulder, and there to relieve him of his load and send him back. It was cold clear weather, and the wind was not too strong. Presently, however, it began to freshen, and after they had gained a few hundred feet it was Tejbir who showed the first signs of weakness. He collapsed entirely, and had to be relieved of his cylinders and sent back. The height was about 26,000 feet, the highest point which any native had yet reached.

In order to move more quickly, Mr. Finch and Captain Bruce dispensed with the rope. The rocks were quite easy, and at 26,500 feet they had passed two admirable sites for a camp. But the wind was steadily increasing

in force, and they were compelled to leave the ridge
and traverse out across the great north face. This
was bad luck, for the ridge was easy climbing and the
face was not. The stratification of the rocks was most
awkward, and it was hard to find any good footholds.
The climbers were unroped, and it was a severe test
of Captain Bruce, who had had no mountaineering
experience to give him confidence. Sometimes they
were on treacherous slopes, sometimes on more treacherous snow, and they often had to cross heaps of scree
that moved with every step. They stopped occasionally to replace an empty cylinder of oxygen with
a new one, each of which meant five pounds off their
load. Presently the aneroid gave their height as
27,000 feet. They now ceased traversing, and began
to climb straight upward to a point on the North-East
ridge, half way between the shoulder and the summit.
Soon they were at 27,300 feet, and the top of Everest
was the only mountain they could see without looking
down. The peaks which had seemed so formidable
from the glacier had now sunk into insignificant humps.
They were 1,700 feet below the summit, well within
half a mile of it, and they could distinguish stones
and a patch of scree just under its highest point.

But it was very clear that they could go no farther.

Weak with hunger and the anxiety and labours of the past forty-eight hours, it was plain to Mr. Finch that if they went on even for another 500 feet they would not both get back alive. Like wise and brave men they decided to retreat. It was now about midday, and for greater safety they roped together. At first they followed their old tracks, and then moved towards the North ridge at a point higher than where they had left it. They reached the ridge at two o'clock, and there reduced their burden by dumping four oxygen cylinders at a place to which future climbers could be directed.

The weather was getting worse. A violent wind from the west was bringing up mist, but happily there was no snow. Half an hour later they reached their camp of the night before, where they found Tejbir sound asleep, wrapped up in all the three sleeping-bags. The porters from the North Col were a mile below, and Tejbir was instructed to go down with them. The rest of the descent was a nightmare. The knees of the climbers knocked together, and their limbs did not seem to respond to the direction of the brain. Often they staggered and slipped, and often they were forced to sit down. But at four o'clock in the afternoon they reached the North Col. Happily they still felt famished; they had not yet reached the limit of a man's strength when hunger vanishes. At the North Col they had hot tea and spaghetti, and three-quarters of an hour later they started off for Camp 3 in the company of Captain Noel. The journey was made in record time—forty minutes— and at 5.30 they had reached Camp 3, having descended since midday 6,000 feet.

That evening made amends for the long hours of famine. " Four whole quails, truffled in *paté de foie gras*, followed by nine sausages, left me asking for more. The last I remember of that long day was going to sleep, warm in the depths of our wonderful sleeping-bag, with the remains of a tin of toffee tucked away in the crook of my elbow."

Captain Bruce's feet were badly frost-bitten, but Mr. Finch had come off scot-free, which was neither more nor less than a physical miracle.

As Captain Bruce, on the way down to the base camp, turned to take his last close view of Everest, his farewell was : " Just you wait, old thing. You will be for it soon." It was the logical conclusion. He and Mr. Finch had got to 27,300 feet after exertions and deprivations which might well have unfitted a man for the ascent of the Rigi. These misfortunes were accidental and not inevitable. The value—the superlative value—of oxygen had been abundantly proved. It may be fairly said that the 1922 expedition, though it had not set foot on the summit, had solved the secret of Everest. The mountain could almost certainly be climbed, provided a little luck attended the climbers. Now that the quality of the native porters has been proved, there seems no reason why, with the help of oxygen, a sixth camp could not be arranged on one of the flat places under 27,000 feet which Mr. Finch noted. A night in such a camp would be no more trying than a night at 25,000 feet. If the climbers, starting from 27,000 feet, and, after a good night, fell in with reasonable weather, there seems little doubt that the remaining 2,000 feet could be ascended and the peak conquered, with a good prospect of a safe return on the same day to the North Col. There remains, of course, the possibility of physical breakdown, such as happened to Major Morshead and Tejbir. But against this may be set the fact that Mr. Mallory, Mr. Somervell, Mr. Norton, Mr. Finch, and Captain Bruce, at great altitudes and after severe physical labour, were not specially distressed, and suffered no bad effects afterwards.

The conquest of Everest will always remain one of the most difficult adventures which man can undertake. But it is a reasonable adventure, and not a piece of crazy foolhardiness, which could only succeed by the help of the one chance in a million. The two reconnaissance expeditions have shown that for its achievement every available human resource is necessary. But granted the utilization of these resources, and the possibility, which our familiarity with the lower slopes may soon permit, of waiting upon a spell of kindly weather, the ultimate conquest would seem to be assured. The secret of Everest has been solved. We know now that there is a way to the top, and we know what that way is.*

* The narratives on which the above account is based will be found in *Mount Everest : The Reconnaissance* (Edwin Arnold, 1921), and the papers by Mr. Mallory and Mr. Finch in the *Alpine Journal* of November, 1922.

THE END.

Lightning Source UK Ltd.
Milton Keynes UK
UKOW03f2132200117
292509UK00004B/89/P